150 Best
Spiralizer
Recipes

150 Best
Spiralizer
Recipes

Marilyn Haugen & Jennifer Williams

Robert
ROSE

For complete cataloguing information, see page 224.

Disclaimer
The recipes in this book have been carefully tested by our kitchen and our tasters. To the best of our knowledge, they are safe and nutritious for ordinary use and users. For those people with food or other allergies, or who have special food requirements or health issues, please read the suggested contents of each recipe carefully and determine whether or not they may create a problem for you. All recipes are used at the risk of the consumer. Consumers should always consult their spiralizer manufacturer's manual for recommended procedures and cooking times.

We cannot be responsible for any hazards, loss or damage that may occur as a result of any recipe use.

For those with special needs, allergies, requirements or health problems, in the event of any doubt, please contact your medical adviser prior to the use of any recipe.

Design and production: Kevin Cockburn/PageWave Graphics Inc.
Editor: Sue Sumeraj
Recipe editor: Jennifer MacKenzie
Proofreader: Kelly Jones
Indexer: Gillian Watts
Photographer: Colin Erricson
Associate photographer: Matt Johannsson
Food stylist: Michael Elliott
Prop stylist: Charlene Erricson

Cover image: Parsnip Spaghetti with Pine Nut Basil Pesto (page 211)

Spiralizer prep images background: © iStockphoto.com/Antonel

The publisher gratefully acknowledges the financial support of our publishing program by the Government of Canada through the Canada Book Fund.

Published by Robert Rose Inc.
120 Eglinton Avenue East, Suite 800, Toronto, Ontario, Canada M4P 1E2
Tel: (416) 322-6552 Fax: (416) 322-6936
www.robertrose.ca

Printed and bound in Canada

6 7 8 9 10 MI 23 22 21 20 19 18 17 16

FSC MIX
Paper from responsible sources
FSC® C103567

Contents

Preface

I love kitchen gadgets and accessories and basically any new toy for the kitchen. So when I started seeing spiralizers, spiral slicers, spiral vegetable slicers, spiral cutters or whatever else you would like to call them, I was intrigued. The idea of being able to get more vegetables into my family's diet was compelling. If I could do that in a new and refreshing way, why not? The thought of just adding 2 to 3 cups (500 to 750 mL) more broccoli to my daily diet was not particularly appealing — in fact, for me, thinking of appetizing ways to increase my vegetable servings was incredibly difficult. But if I could use vegetables to replace the pasta in a dish or make tastier side dishes and entrées, I was definitely going to experiment.

Most of the recipes I tried early on involved using zucchini to make noodles. They were very quick and easy, and the results were delicious and satisfying. But I soon realized there was so much more I could do with this handy little gadget. After all, we don't eat a pasta dish every day (at least, I don't). Jazzing up a salad seemed simple enough: I wanted to try new types of salads with a variety of ingredients. But what if I could apply spiralizing to create innovative entrées and side dishes, or updated versions of classic favorites? Now *that* got my creative juices going.

After experimenting with many different options (some outstanding and some that were seriously questionable), I came up with numerous easy, inviting and delicious dishes that I was eager to try out on friends. It was a great excuse to host dinner parties! Not only did we have fun get-togethers, but I got valuable feedback for my recipes.

The next test was my college-age daughter — a valuable and brutally honest critic. I imagined she would be dismayed by the mere thought that I had changed some of her longtime favorites. But she loved the dishes I created for her and was excited about this easy way to eat healthier.

The result is this book, which features creative recipes for salads, soups, main dishes and sides. It includes many updated classics and comfort food recipes, but it also expands the boundaries of what you can do with fresh produce and your spiralizer. I have included recipes for gluten-free, paleo, vegetarian and vegan, and raw food diets. (And many of these dishes work for two or more of these diets.) But people who are not following a specific diet will also enjoy these dishes.

The shapes, textures and flavors are appealing to a variety of taste buds.

With your spiralizer and this cookbook at hand, you will be able to quickly and easily add variety to your diet and impress your family and friends with delicious, beautiful, nutritious and extremely satisfying dishes.

If you enjoy the recipes and tips you read here, stop by my blog, www.FoodThymes.com, to see what new recipes and gadgets I am playing with at the moment. While you are there, feel free to share your own spiralizing and foodie experiences — the camaraderie just makes this whole adventure so much more fun.

Now let's start spiralizing!

— *Marilyn Haugen*

Acknowledgments

I cannot begin to thank the many people who made this book possible without first and foremost giving my heartfelt thanks to my mother. Her endless love and encouragement taught me that you can accomplish anything. Without that, this book would not have been possible. I wish she was here now to see it come to life.

My grandparents gave me an appreciation for a variety of vegetables and home-cooked meals. I so enjoyed romping around their small farm when I was young. Every day we enjoyed a bounty of delicious fresh vegetables in many different dishes.

My aunt and godmother, through her cooking and baking, showed me that zucchini was not an "icky" vegetable if you learn how to use it correctly.

The support of my dear friend Karla Rabusch continues to keep me motivated and excited about my new cookbook ventures. On a recent visit to her home in San Francisco, the importance of eating lighter was reaffirmed as I walked the hills of that city. The variety of delicious foods we ate and the experiences of the neighborhoods inspired a number of recipes in this book.

Special thanks to my taste-testers, especially my wonderful daughter, Natalie, for endlessly tasting recipes and giving me valuable feedback, support and encouragement.

I also appreciate the contributions from Jennifer Williams and am grateful that her experience led to this book's development.

My sincere appreciation to Bob Dees, my publisher, who gave me the opportunity to share these recipes. My editor,

Sue Sumeraj, is always outstanding to work with. She has extraordinary insight into what will make a great experience for our readers. I continue to learn so much from both Sue and Jennifer MacKenzie, a recipe developer and author, about what makes an exceptional recipe and cookbook.

Many thanks to Kevin Cockburn of PageWave Graphics for the wonderful design; to the team at Colin Erricson Photography for the stunning photographs; and to all of the outstanding professionals at Robert Rose who made this process a truly enjoyable and successful experience.

Spiralizing Basics

If you are looking for a new twist on healthy cooking and more tantalizing ways to eat vegetables and fruits, then spiralizing is for you. The beauty of spiralizing vegetables, particularly if you are substituting them for traditional wheat pasta, is that you can eliminate gluten, reduce your caloric intake and lower your intake of carbohydrates.

Using a spiral vegetable cutter is a fast and easy way to cut vegetables (and some fruits) into a variety of noodle shapes. The long, appealing slices make a perfect healthy alternative to traditional pasta, they are ideal for stir-fries, soups, salads and side dishes, and they make beautiful garnishes.

About Spiralizers

A spiralizer is a small kitchen gadget that makes cutting fruits and vegetables into long, thin slices an extremely easy, fast, streamlined process. There is a huge variety of these gadgets available today at kitchen stores, big-box retailers and online, with new versions frequently being released.

There are two basic types of spiralizers — a large one that sits on your countertop and a smaller handheld one — but each brand offers its own benefits and features that you will want to consider before purchase.

A countertop spiralizer features three or four cutting blades for noodles of different sizes. You insert the produce into the spiralizer either horizontally or vertically (depending on the brand), between the blades and a spinning wheel with prongs. Then you rotate the handle, or turn the spiralizer on, and watch the beautiful spiral cuts come out the opposite end.

While this unit is fairly large — about 12 by 6 inches (30 by 15 cm) — it offers a couple of distinct advantages: you have more leverage for spiralizing vegetables and fruits, particularly those that are denser and tougher to cut, and the hand crank keeps your fingers away from the blades. You can easily change blades by sliding them in and out. The unit also packs up nicely for storage in smaller spaces.

A handheld spiralizer has no handle to turn. The produce fits into the cone at one end and the cutting motion is achieved by turning the vegetable or fruit with one hand while holding the spiralizer with the other. This compact tool typically features two cutting blades. It is a good option if you are tight on space.

Spiralizer Blades

The type of noodles you are able to cut will vary depending on the type and brand of spiralizer you use. Because every brand seems to have different names for their cutting blades, the recipes in this book focus on the resulting size of the noodles:

- *Fine strands:* Very thin noodles similar to angel hair pasta (about 1.2 by 2 mm).
- *Thin strands:* Noodles similar to spaghetti (about 3 by 3 mm).
- *Medium strands:* Noodles similar to fettuccine (about 4 by 6 mm).
- *Wide ribbons:* Noodles similar to pappardelle or egg noodles, or much larger, depending on the vegetable and the desired result (about 2.5 mm by up to 75 mm).

Examination of your cutting blades and perusal of your user's manual should make it clear which of these sizes you are able to make. If you are eager to try a recipe but don't have the type of blade necessary to make the specified cuts, in most cases you can substitute a different noodle size; just keep in mind that you may have to adjust the cooking time (where applicable).

Other Useful Tools

Aside from your spiralizer and some standard pots and pans, there are a few other kitchen tools that you will find handy when preparing the recipes in this book.

- *Large sharp knife:* The best tool for cutting off the ends of your produce and peeling hard, dense vegetables.
- *Vegetable peeler:* Makes the task of peeling vegetables and fruits much easier.
- *Strainer:* Useful if you want to drain some of the moisture from your produce before adding it to your dishes. You can also pat spiralized fruits and vegetables dry with paper towels, or drain them using cheesecloth or a large nut milk bag.
- *Parchment paper:* Ideal for lining baking sheets when you are baking spiralized fruits and vegetables, as it prevents them from sticking to the baking sheet and breaking.
- *Kitchen gloves:* A good idea when you're handling beets, carrots and other vegetables that can stain your hands.
- *Garlic press:* Makes mincing garlic a snap.
- *Food processor:* Used in some recipes to process ingredients, such as nuts or cauliflower, or to blend sauces and salad dressings.
- *Mortar and pestle:* Handy for making a paste for salad dressings and for grinding spices.

The Spiralizing Pantry

The most important components of your spiralizing pantry will, of course, be a colorful array of fresh, ripe vegetables and fruits. Always use the best produce you can find. The quality of the produce will determine the quality of the final dish. For best results, choose:

- Fully ripened vegetables and fruits (unless otherwise noted).
- Produce that is in season in your area. Not only will the flavor and texture be better, but local vegetables and fruits often cost less.
- The straightest possible vegetables and fruits.
- Medium-size vegetables that will fit easily in your spiralizer.
- Produce that is at least $1\frac{1}{2}$ inches (4 cm) in length and width.
- Produce that is firm and does not have soft, mushy flesh.
- Produce that does not have large pits or seeds (with the exceptions of butternut squash, cucumbers and zucchini).

Add to your pantry some oils, vinegars, broths and condiments, and some herbs, seasonings and other flavorings, and you're ready to start spiralizing!

The Best Vegetables and Fruits for Spiralizing

Zucchini is a very common substitute for conventional wheat pasta in recipes. However, there is a wide variety of produce you can spiralize. The following fruits and vegetables have given me the best results and are used in the recipes in this book. All measurements are approximate. Wash all produce before use.

APPLES

I have had the best results with Fuji, Gala, Cameo and Honey Crisp apples if I want a sweeter taste, and Pink Lady and Braeburn for a tarter taste. Apples should be firm and crisp, not soft.

Before Spiralizing
- Remove the stems and core the apples.
- You can peel the skin, but it is not necessary. Leaving the skin on will reduce breakage of the strands.

After Spiralizing
- Apples start to discolor very quickly, so if you are not using the strands immediately, either spray them lightly with lemon juice or cover them with a mixture of 2 cups (500 mL) water and 1 tbsp (15 mL) lemon juice. Drain before use.

Ideal Cuts
- Thin strands
- Medium strands

> 3 to 4 medium apples = 1 lb (500 g)
>
> 1 medium apple = 1 cup (250 mL) spiralized

BEETS

Red, orange and yellow beets work equally well. Choose beets that are 3 inches (7.5 cm) or less in diameter, as larger beets can be fibrous in the center. You may want to wear kitchen gloves when handling red beets so you don't stain your hands. Beet leaves can be washed and used in salads or cooked. Remove the red stems before use.

Before Spiralizing
- Remove the stems and cut the ends flat.
- You can peel the skin, if desired. If you keep the skin on, scrub it well to remove any fibers and blemishes.

Ideal Cuts
- All

> 3 to 4 medium beets = 1 lb (500 g)
>
> 1½ medium beets = 1 cup (250 mL) spiralized

BELL PEPPERS

Green, red, orange and yellow peppers work equally well. You can use what is recommended in the recipe or mix it up depending upon what colors you want to use or what is available.

Before Spiralizing
- Remove the stems.
- You can core the peppers, if desired, but the best results will be achieved if you remove the seeds and the white connective tissue after spiralizing.

Ideal Cut
- Wide ribbons

2 to 3 medium peppers = 1 lb (500 g)

1 medium pepper = 1½ cups (375 mL) spiralized

BUTTERNUT SQUASH

Use only the neck of the squash. The neck should be at least 4 inches (10 cm) long. Save the squash bulb to use in a variety of recipes.

Before Spiralizing
- Peel the squash neck, making sure to remove not only the outer skin, but also the next layer of lighter flesh so you will spiralize only the darker orange–colored flesh.
- Trim the peeled squash neck to 4 inches (10 cm) long, with the ends cut flat.

Ideal Cuts
- Thin strands
- Medium strands
- Wide ribbons

Butternut squash sizes vary greatly

4-inch (10 cm) long by 3-inch (7.5 cm) diameter neck = 2 cups (500 mL) spiralized

BROCCOLI STEMS

Choose heads of broccoli with stems that are relatively straight and at least 1½ inches (4 cm) in diameter. You may be able to find just individual stems at your grocer if you do not want to use the florets.

Before Spiralizing
- Peel the stems to make them straighter.

Ideal Cuts
- Fine strands
- Thin strands

1 medium head broccoli, stalk only = 1½ cups (375 mL) spiralized

1 medium head broccoli, florets only = 3½ cups (875 mL)

CABBAGE

1 medium cabbage = 2 lbs (1 kg)

1 medium cabbage = 8 cups (2 L) spiralized

Most varieties of cabbage with tightly packed leaves work well. The cabbage should feel heavy for its size. I have had the best results with red and green cabbage. Use the type that is recommended in the recipe.

Before Spiralizing

- Peel off the outer leaves and trim the ends flat.
- Depending on the size of your cabbage and spiralizer, you may need to cut the cabbage in half to make it easier to spiralize.

Ideal Cuts

- Medium strands
- Wide ribbons

CARROTS

8 medium carrots = 1 lb (500 g)

2 medium carrots = 1 cup (250 mL) spiralized

Use whole, not baby carrots. Orange carrots are the most common variety, but any color will work. You may want to wear kitchen gloves when handling carrots so you don't stain your hands.

Before Spiralizing

- Peel the carrots, remove the stems and cut the ends flat.
- Cut the carrots into appropriate lengths to fit in your spiralizer, if necessary.

Ideal Cuts

- All

CELERY ROOTS (CELERIAC)

2 medium celery roots = 1 lb (500 g)

1 medium celery root = 1 cup (250 mL) spiralized

Choose celery roots that are about 3 to 4 inches (7.5 to 10 cm) in diameter.

Before Spiralizing

- Peel the celery roots and cut the ends flat. The best way to peel a celery root is to cut off one end and then place the celery root, cut end down, on a cutting board. Holding the uncut end and using a downward cutting motion, use a large sharp knife to remove the skin. Then cut the remaining end flat.

After Spiralizing

- Rinse the celery root strands.
- Celery root starts to discolor very quickly, so if you are not using the strands immediately, either spray them lightly with lemon juice or cover them with a mixture of 2 cups

(500 mL) water and 1 tbsp (15 mL) lemon juice. Drain before use.

Ideal Cuts
- Thin strands
- Medium strands

CUCUMBERS

3 medium cucumbers = 2 lbs (1 kg)

1 medium cucumber = 1 cup (250 mL) spiralized

Choose cucumbers that are firm and have no soft spots when you depress the skin with your thumb. They should be dark green and feel heavy for their size. Thinner cucumbers are better for spiralizing because they will have fewer seeds and be firmer inside.

Before Spiralizing
- Cut the ends flat.
- You can peel the skin, if desired, but I have the best results with keeping it on.
- Cut the cucumbers into appropriate lengths to fit in your spiralizer, if necessary.

After Spiralizing
- Cucumber ribbons should be drained or patted dry with a paper towel before they are added to your dish. You can also sprinkle the ribbons lightly with salt and then let them drain in a colander for up to 30 minutes; rinse and pat dry before using. This removes the water more thoroughly than just patting the ribbons dry. It is a useful practice for dishes where you are using more than one cucumber or are combining them with a variety of other vegetables and do not want the additional liquid.

Ideal Cut
- Wide ribbons

DAIKON RADISH

1 medium radish (about 7 inches/ 18 cm long) = 12 oz (375 g)

1 medium radish = ⅔ cup (150 mL) spiralized

Choose daikon radishes that are crisp (firm), shiny and blemish-free. If your daikon comes with the stems and leaves, cut off the leaves before storing; they should be stored separately from the root. Daikon leaves can be washed and cooked in a variety of recipes. Store your daikon root in the refrigerator for up to 3 days, wrapped tightly in plastic wrap as it is very odorous.

Before Spiralizing
- Peel the radishes and cut the ends flat. (If you prefer, you can skip peeling them, but in that case they will need to

be well scrubbed before use. I find you get the best results with peeling, because you can make the radishes more even before spiralizing.)

- Cut the radishes into appropriate lengths to fit in your spiralizer, if necessary.

Ideal Cuts
- Thin strands
- Medium strands
- Wide ribbons

DELICATA SQUASH

2 medium delicata squash = 1 lb (500 g)

1 medium delicata squash = 1½ cups (375 mL) spiralized

Squash sizes can vary substantially. Choose squash that are shorter in length, or cut them to an ideal length. Shorter squash will make removing the seeds easier.

Before Spiralizing
- Cut the ends flat.
- You do not need to peel delicata squash, but if your squash has a thicker skin than you prefer, you can peel it before spiralizing. You can easily check the thickness of the skin once you have cut off the ends of the squash.
- After cutting off the ends, use a long spoon to scoop out the seeds.

Ideal Cuts
- Medium strands
- Wide ribbons

JICAMA

1 medium jicama = 12 oz (375 g)

1 medium jicama = 2 cups (500 mL) spiralized

Choose jicama that are round and blemish-free and have no wrinkling (which suggests lower water content) or soft spots. Ideal jicama are crisp and juicy. They should feel heavy for their size, indicating high water content.

Before Spiralizing
- Peel the jicama and cut the ends flat.

After Spiralizing
- Jicama have a high water content. The strands or ribbons should be drained or patted dry with a paper towel before they are added to your dish.

Ideal Cuts
- Thin strands
- Medium strands
- Wide ribbons

KOHLRABI

Choose kohlrabi that feel heavy for their size. Lighter kohlrabi are over-ripened, can be woody inside and will not be as crisp and sweet. Kohlrabi leaves are delightful mixed in with other greens or seasoned and cooked as a side dish.

Before Spiralizing
• Peel the kohlrabi and cut the ends flat.

Ideal Cuts
• All

3 to
4 medium
kohlrabi = 1 lb
(500 g)

1 medium
kohlrabi
= ¾ cup
(175 mL)
spiralized

ONIONS

Choose onions that are firm and dry and have a lustrous outer skin. When you hold an onion in your palm and squeeze slightly, it should not feel watery and soft inside. There is very little, if any, difference in taste or sharpness between traditional yellow and white onions. Sweet onions, such as Walla Walla or Vidalia, have a sweeter and much less sharp taste. Use the type of onion that is recommended in the recipe.

Onions have a tendency to spray some juice while they are being spiralized. Take care to protect your eyes and other surfaces.

Before Spiralizing
• Peel the onion and cut the ends flat.

Ideal Cuts
• All

4 to
5 medium
onions = 1 lb
(500 g)

1½ medium
onions
= 1 cup
(250 mL)
spiralized

PARSNIPS

Before Spiralizing
• Peel the parsnips, remove the stems and cut the ends flat.
• Cut the parsnips into appropriate lengths to fit in your spiralizer, if necessary.

Ideal Cuts
• All

4 medium
parsnips = 1 lb
(500 g)

1½ medium
parsnips
= 1 cup
(250 mL)
spiralized

PEARS

I have had the best results with green or red Anjou pears. Pears should be firm and crisp, not soft.

Before Spiralizing
- Remove the stems and core the pears.
- You can peel the skin, but it is not necessary. Leaving the skin on will reduce breakage of the strands.

After Spiralizing
- Handle the pear strands or ribbons carefully, as they break easily.
- Pears start to discolor very quickly, so if you are not using the strands immediately, either spray them lightly with lemon juice or cover them with a mixture of 2 cups (500 mL) water and 1 tbsp (15 mL) lemon juice. Drain before use.

Ideal Cuts
- Medium strands
- Wide ribbons

3 to
4 medium
pears = 1 lb
(500 g)

1 medium
pear = ¾ cup
(175 mL)
spiralized

PLANTAINS

Choose plantains that are green (unripened) and relatively straight. Green plantains are firmer and work better in the spiralizer. If the strands break into smaller pieces, that is fine.

Before Spiralizing
- Peel the plantains and cut the ends flat.

Ideal Cuts
- Thin strands

3 medium
plantains =
1 lb (500 g)

1 medium
plantain
= ¾ cup
(175 mL)

POTATOES

Russet potatoes, small red-skinned potatoes and yellow-fleshed (Yukon Gold) potatoes work well. For best results, they should be at least $1\frac{1}{2}$ inches (4 cm) in both diameter and length.

Before Spiralizing
- Peel the potatoes and cut the ends flat.

3 to
4 medium
white
potatoes =
1 lb (500 g)

7 to 9 small
red-skinned
or yellow-
fleshed
potatoes =
1 lb (500 g)

After Spiralizing

- Potatoes start to discolor very quickly, so if you are not using the strands immediately, either spray them lightly with lemon juice or cover them with a mixture of 2 cups (500 mL) water and 1 tbsp (15 mL) lemon juice. Drain before use.

Ideal Cuts

- All

RED RADISHES

Radishes can be spiralized only with a countertop spiralizer, not the handheld type, as their small size puts your fingertips at risk of touching the blades of handheld versions. Large radishes — at least $1\frac{1}{2}$ inches (4 cm) in diameter and 3 inches (7.5 cm) in length — are best for spiralizing.

Before Spiralizing

- Remove the stems and cut the ends flat.

Ideal Cuts

- Medium strands
- Wide ribbons

RUTABAGAS

Choose rutabagas that are smooth and heavy. Colors can range from beige to purple; the color does not indicate ripeness. Any variety works well. Most store-bought rutabagas come with a waxy coating to prevent them from drying out during transit. This coating will be removed when you peel them.

Before Spiralizing

- Peel the rutabagas and cut the ends flat. The best way to peel a rutabaga is to cut off one end and then place the rutabaga, cut end down, on a cutting board. Holding the uncut end and using a downward cutting motion, use a large sharp knife to remove the skin. Then cut the remaining end flat.

Ideal Cuts

- Thin strands
- Medium strands

SWEET POTATOES

Choose sweet potatoes that are firm, smooth-skinned and blemish-free. They should be evenly shaped, without any crooked parts. Sweet potatoes can vary substantially in size; select those that are less than 9 inches (23 cm) in length and 3 inches (7.5 cm) in diameter.

Occasionally, the terms "yam" and "sweet potato" are used interchangeably, but these are, in fact, completely different vegetables. Make sure you are purchasing sweet potatoes and not yams.

Before Spiralizing
• Peel the sweet potatoes and cut the ends flat.

Ideal Cuts
• Fine strands
• Thin strands
• Medium strands

3 medium sweet potatoes (about 5 inches/ 12.5 cm long by 2 inches/ 5 cm in diameter) = 1 lb (500 g)

~~~

1 medium sweet potato = 1 cup (250 mL) spiralized

TURNIPS

Choose smaller turnips, about 3 inches (7.5 cm) in diameter, for sweeter and more tender results. They should feel heavy for their size and should not have any soft spots. Turnips come in a variety of shapes and colors, none of which indicates ripeness or taste. Any variety works well.

Before Spiralizing
• Peel the turnips and cut the ends flat.

Ideal Cut
• Thin strands

5 small turnips = 1 lb (500 g)

~~~

1½ small turnips = 1 cup (250 mL) spiralized

YELLOW SUMMER SQUASH

Choose squash that are relatively straight and at least 1½ inches (4 cm) in diameter. They should not have any soft spots or bruising.

Before Spiralizing
• Cut the ends flat.
• You do not need to peel the squash.

Ideal Cuts
• All

2 to 3 medium squash = 1 lb (500 g)

~~~

1 medium squash = 1 cup (250 mL) spiralized

▶ ZUCCHINI

Choose zucchini that are relatively straight and at least
1½ inches (4 cm) in diameter. They should not have any
soft spots or bruising.

Before Spiralizing
- Cut the ends flat.
- You do not need to peel the zucchini.

Ideal Cuts
- All

Oils

Olive oil is used in many of the recipes in this book. The high
quality and superior taste of extra virgin olive oil make it the
best choice for salads and other recipes that are not cooked;
however, since extra virgin olive oil has a relatively low smoke
point, regular olive oil is a better (and less expensive) choice
for recipes that are cooked.

Virgin coconut oil, peanut oil, sunflower oil, sesame oil,
grapeseed oil and hemp oil are also good options to have on hand.

Vinegars

Vinegar can impact the texture, color, flavor and thickness
of dishes, adding acidity and sourness that can increase our
enjoyment of our food. There are many types of vinegar, each of
which has its own unique flavor. The vinegars used in this book
include balsamic vinegar, cider vinegar, red wine vinegar, white
wine vinegar and rice vinegar. If you are unsure which ones to
have on hand, start with whichever one is used in a recipe you
want to make, then expand your pantry provisions from there.

Broths

Chicken, vegetable and beef broths are wonderful choices for
simmering vegetable noodles, and they add depth of flavor to
soups and simmering meats. You can make your broth from
scratch, buy ready-to-use broth or use bouillon cubes. Some
recipes recommend using reduced-sodium broths either because
a large amount of broth is called for or because other ingredients
contribute sodium to the recipe. Using the type of broth

specified in the recipe (whether regular or reduced-sodium) will give you the best balance of flavors in the finished dish.

Condiments

Versatile condiments that will add zest and flavor to your dishes include Dijon mustard, Sriracha, tamari, Worcestershire sauce, honey and maple syrup. Stock your pantry with a variety of condiments that suit your taste, as they can be used to enhance many dishes.

Herbs, Seasonings and Flavorings

When adding fresh or dried herbs, seasonings and flavorings, remember that a little goes a long way. Always use the amount specified in the recipe for the best flavor and consistency. If you are confident in your cooking skills and experience, then you may want to adjust the amounts, but do so only in small increments.

If a recipe calls for fresh herbs but you only have dried herbs on hand, the general rule of thumb is to use one-third the amount of dried herbs. For example, if the recipe calls for 3 tbsp (45 mL) chopped fresh parsley, you can substitute 1 tbsp (15 mL) dried parsley. Keep in mind that dried herbs will not have the same purity of flavor as fresh herbs.

Get Ready, Get Set, Spiralize!

Once you've decided on a recipe you want to prepare, scan the ingredient list to make sure you have everything you need on hand. For best results, purchase fresh vegetables and fruits just before you want to use them, or at the most, 2 to 3 days ahead.

You will have the most success with your dishes if you have all of the ingredients prepped and ready to go before you start following the recipe steps. In these recipes, the cooking times for the vegetables are often quite short, and having the other ingredients ready will help you avoid overcooked, soggy noodles.

Always add the ingredients in the order listed and according to the recipe directions.

Quick Tips for Best Results

- Use the manual included with your spiralizer for instructions on how to assemble it, if necessary, and how to achieve the best results. The manufacturer is the expert on how to use its spiralizer.
- Choose thick, firm, straight vegetables and fruits.
- Select vegetables and fruits that are not overly large. If they are too large, you will not be able to handle them as nimbly and they may not fit properly in your spiralizer.
- Use produce without a pit or a large quantity of seeds. For those with seeds, such as cucumbers, the thinner they are, the better they will spiralize.
- Always use fully ripe vegetables and fruits, unless otherwise indicated in the recipe. For superior results, use the best quality you can find.
- Wash all produce and make sure it is dry before use.
- Position your vegetable or fruit as straight as possible in the spiralizer.
- Measure ingredients carefully for optimal results.
- When cooking vegetables, do not overcrowd them in the pan or pot.
- Clean your spiralizer immediately after use. A kitchen brush is the best tool for this task.
- After washing the cutters, dry the blades carefully to prevent rust or tarnishing.

Safety Note

As with any cutting tool, the blade edges on a spiralizer are very sharp. Be careful when cutting produce and when cleaning the cutters.

Gluten-Free Recipes

Quick Celery Root Slaw with Capers

This tangy and zesty celery root slaw is wonderful as an accompaniment to fish and chicken dishes. Ready in no time, it is easy to make for a weeknight side dish.

MAKES 6 SERVINGS		

Tips

Use a paring knife to peel the skin off the celery root. You want to cut down to the creamy white flesh, removing the skin and darker internal layer. Depending on the size or awkward shape of your celery root, you may want to cut the root in half. Keep in mind that it needs to fit in your spiralizer.

This slaw can be stored in an airtight container in the refrigerator for up to 2 days.

1	large celery root, peeled and ends cut flat	1
¾ cup	mayonnaise	175 mL
¼ cup	whole milk	60 mL
¼ cup	drained capers	60 mL
2 tbsp	Dijon mustard	30 mL
2 tbsp	freshly squeezed lemon juice	30 mL
1 tsp	kosher salt	5 mL

1. Using a spiralizer, cut celery root into thin strands.
2. In a large bowl, combine mayonnaise, milk, capers, mustard, lemon juice and salt. Add celery root and mix well.

Variation

Instead of the capers, cut a tart green apple, such as a Granny Smith, into thin strands and add to the celery root.

Curly Fruits and Greens with Feta and Cranberries

This refreshing salad has an inviting and unique combination of ingredients that will dance across your taste buds.

MAKES 2 SERVINGS

Tips

To toast chopped walnuts, spread them on a rimmed baking sheet and toast in a 350°F (180°C) oven for 5 to 8 minutes, tossing once partway through, until fragrant but not darkened.

The dressing makes about ¼ cup (60 mL). You can make a larger quantity and store it in an airtight container in the refrigerator for up to 3 days.

For added color and a slightly tarter taste, leave the skin on the green apple.

Salad

1	kohlrabi, peeled and ends cut flat	1
1	green apple, peeled and cored	1
2½ cups	baby arugula	625 mL
¼ cup	crumbled feta cheese	60 mL
2 tbsp	dried cranberries	30 mL
2 tbsp	chopped walnuts, toasted (see tip, at left)	30 mL

Dressing

1 tbsp	liquid honey	15 mL
1½ tbsp	extra virgin olive oil	22 mL
1½ tsp	red wine vinegar	7 mL
1½ tsp	grainy Dijon mustard	7 mL
Pinch	kosher salt (optional)	Pinch
Pinch	freshly ground black pepper (optional)	Pinch

1. *Salad:* Using a spiralizer, cut kohlrabi and apple into thin strands.
2. Place arugula in a serving bowl. Add kohlrabi and apple strands on top. Sprinkle with cheese, cranberries and walnuts.
3. *Dressing:* In a bowl, whisk together honey, oil, vinegar and mustard. Season with salt and pepper, if using.
4. Pour dressing over salad and toss to coat.

Zesty Noodle Salad with Corn and Tomatoes

This salad is great for a light lunch or as a side salad, and the reds, greens and yellows make a festive presentation for guests, too.

Tips

Choose zucchini that are straight and fairly even in diameter. This will make it easier to spiral-cut them evenly.

If fresh corn is not available, you can thaw a 12-oz (375 g) package of frozen corn to use in its place.

5	zucchini, ends cut flat	5
1½ cups	fresh corn kernels (about 2 cobs)	375 mL
2 cups	cherry tomatoes, halved	500 mL
1	clove garlic, minced	1
½ tsp	kosher salt	2 mL
¼ tsp	granulated sugar	1 mL
¼ cup	white wine vinegar or champagne vinegar	60 mL
¼ cup	extra virgin olive oil	60 mL
¼ cup	sesame oil	60 mL
3 tbsp	coarsely chopped basil leaves (optional)	45 mL
½ cup	shaved Parmesan cheese	125 mL

1. Using a spiralizer, cut zucchini into thin strands. Place in a serving bowl and add corn and tomatoes.

2. In a 2-cup (500 mL) container with a tight seal, combine garlic, salt, sugar, vinegar, olive oil and sesame oil. Seal tightly and shake vigorously to combine.

3. Pour dressing over salad and toss to coat. Let stand for 5 to 10 minutes or until zucchini is softened and flavors are blended. Sprinkle with basil, if desired. Sprinkle with cheese.

Korean Sweet Potato Salad

This salad is similar to the traditional Korean dish *japchae*, but uses fresh sweet potatoes instead of the usual noodles made with sweet potato starch.

Tips

You can use the spiralizer to cut the onion, too. The medium blade works best here. Cut the resulting strands into smaller (4-inch/10 cm) lengths.

Toast sesame seeds in a small skillet over medium-high heat for 3 to 4 minutes or until fragrant.

3	carrots, peeled and ends cut flat	3
2	large sweet potatoes, peeled and ends cut flat	2
10 tsp	sesame oil, divided	50 mL
¼ cup	tamari	60 mL
1 tbsp	pure maple syrup	15 mL
1	onion, thinly sliced	1
4 oz	baby portobello mushrooms, sliced	125 g
8	small kale leaves, stems removed, chopped	8
1	red bell pepper, thinly sliced	1
2 tbsp	toasted sesame seeds (see tip, at left)	30 mL
4	green onions, finely sliced	4

1. Using a spiralizer, cut carrots and sweet potatoes into thin strands, keeping them separate. Cut carrot strands into 4-inch (10 cm) lengths and set aside.

2. In a large, deep skillet, toss sweet potatoes with 2 tsp (10 mL) oil. Cook over medium-low heat, tossing occasionally, for 5 to 7 minutes or until slightly softened. Transfer to a serving bowl.

3. In a small bowl, combine tamari, 6 tsp (30 mL) oil and maple syrup until well blended. Pour over sweet potatoes and gently toss to coat.

4. In the same skillet, heat the remaining oil over medium-high heat. Add onion and cook, stirring, for 4 to 5 minutes or until translucent. Add carrots, mushrooms, kale and red pepper; cook, tossing, until kale is heated through and slightly softened. Add to serving bowl and sprinkle with sesame seeds and green onions.

Variation

Parsnips or daikon radishes are nice substitutions for the carrots. Or try using 2 carrots and 1 parsnip or radish to change up this salad.

Broccoli Cheese Soup

Treat yourself to a creamy, full-bodied, gratifying bowl of warm, cheesy broccoli soup. Broccoli florets and stems have slightly different flavors and textures, so I use both in this soup.

Tip

If you purchase shredded Cheddar cheese, check the package to make sure it is gluten-free. If you prefer to shred your own cheese, you will need about 5 ounces (150 g).

1	onion, peeled and ends cut flat	1
2	large carrots, peeled and ends cut flat	2
1	head broccoli, florets and stems separated	1
1 tbsp	olive oil	15 mL
5 tbsp	butter, melted, divided	75 mL
1	clove garlic, minced	1
2 tbsp	cornstarch	30 mL
2 cups	ready-to-use reduced-sodium chicken broth	500 mL
2 cups	half-and-half (10%) cream	500 mL
1 tsp	dry mustard	5 mL
1 tsp	kosher salt	5 mL
$\frac{1}{2}$ tsp	freshly ground black pepper	2 mL
$\frac{1}{2}$ tsp	ground ginger	2 mL
$1\frac{1}{4}$ cups	shredded sharp (old) Cheddar cheese, divided	300 mL
	Hot pepper flakes (optional)	

1. Using a spiralizer, cut onion into medium strands. Cut carrots into wide ribbons. Peel broccoli stems and cut into medium strands. Break broccoli florets into $1\frac{1}{2}$-inch (4 cm) pieces.

2. In a medium skillet, heat oil over medium heat. Add carrot ribbons and broccoli strands; cook, stirring, for 3 to 5 minutes or until slightly softened. Transfer to a plate.

3. In the same skillet, melt 1 tbsp (15 mL) butter over medium-high heat. Add onion and cook, stirring, for 4 to 5 minutes or until translucent. Add garlic and cook, stirring, for 30 seconds or until fragrant. Remove from heat and set aside.

Tips

You can use precut broccoli florets and eliminate the stems if you prefer.

Cut off the top of 4 small gluten-free sourdough loaves and scoop the bread out of the core. Serve the warm soup inside the sourdough bowls.

4. In a heavy-bottomed pot, melt the remaining butter over medium heat. Gradually whisk in cornstarch and cook, whisking, for 2 to 3 minutes or until well incorporated. Gradually add broth and cream, stirring continuously. Stir in mustard, salt, black pepper and ginger. Stir in broccoli florets and bring to a simmer. Reduce heat to low, cover and simmer, stirring occasionally, for 20 to 30 minutes or until florets are tender (do not let boil). Stir in reserved onion and carrot and broccoli ribbons. Cover and simmer for 5 to 7 minutes or until vegetables are cooked to desired tenderness. Stir in 1 cup (250 mL) cheese and cook, stirring, for 1 to 2 minutes or until cheese is melted.

5. Serve in soup bowls, topped with remaining cheese. Garnish with hot pepper flakes, if desired.

Mulligatawny Soup

Sweetness and spice and everything nice come together in this satisfying soup with British and Indian origins.

~~~~~~

**MAKES
4 SERVINGS**

Tips

If you want to do away with teary eyes when chopping onions, use your spiralizer to cut them. For this recipe, cut thin or medium strands.

Choose carrots that are as straight as you can find to make it easier to cut them in your spiralizer. Thicker carrots work best, but choose those that are just large, not overgrown. Older, overgrown carrots take on a woody flavor.

▸ **Spice grinder or mortar and pestle**

½ tsp	mustard seeds	2 mL
½ tsp	cumin seeds	2 mL
½ tsp	coriander seeds	2 mL
2 tbsp	vegetable oil	30 mL
1 lb	bone-in, skin-on chicken thighs	500 g
Pinch	kosher salt	Pinch
1	onion, chopped	1
1	stalk celery, chopped	1
3	cloves garlic, minced	3
1 tbsp	finely grated gingerroot	15 mL
1 tbsp	curry powder	15 mL
1	small tomato, chopped	1
½ cup	dried red lentils, rinsed	125 mL
6 cups	ready-to-use reduced-sodium chicken broth	1.5 L
1	sweet potato, peeled and ends cut flat	1
1	carrot, peeled and ends cut flat	1
1	sweet apple (such as Fuji, Sonya or Gala), peeled and cored	1
	Plain Greek yogurt (optional)	
	Chopped fresh cilantro (optional)	

1. In a small skillet over medium-high heat, toast mustard, cumin and coriander seeds for 2 to 3 minutes or until lightly browned and aromatic. Remove from heat and let cool, then finely grind spices in spice grinder or with a mortar and pestle.

2. In a Dutch oven, heat oil over medium heat. Season chicken with salt, add to pot and cook for 8 to 10 minutes, turning once, until golden brown on both sides. Transfer chicken to a plate and set aside.

3. Add onion and celery to the pot and cook, stirring, for 5 to 7 minutes or until onion is translucent. Add ground toasted spices, garlic, ginger and curry powder, stirring to coat vegetables. Return chicken to the pot and stir in tomato, lentils and broth; bring to a simmer. Reduce heat and simmer for 40 to 50 minutes or until lentils are just tender and soup is thickened.

4. Meanwhile, using a spiralizer, cut sweet potato, carrot and apple into medium strands.

5. Transfer chicken to a cutting board and remove bones and skin. Shred meat and return to the pot. Stir in sweet potato, carrot and apple; simmer for 8 to 10 minutes or until vegetables are cooked to desired tenderness. If desired, top each serving with a dollop of yogurt and a pinch of cilantro.

Confetti Veggie Pepperoni Soup

Celebrate a cozy evening at home with this colorful, richly textured confetti soup. Engage your children in making confetti noodles and see if they don't enjoy eating their veggies just a little bit more.

**MAKES
4 SERVINGS**

Variations

Instead of brown rice, use basmati, long-grain white or jasmine rice and reduce the broth to 2½ cups (625 mL).

Add 1 tsp (5 mL) or more horseradish, for a nice kick.

For a vegetarian soup, use ready-to-use reduced-sodium vegetable broth instead of the beef broth and omit the pepperoni.

1 cup	brown rice or brown rice medley	250 mL
3 cups	ready-to-use reduced-sodium beef broth	750 mL
2 tbsp	olive oil	30 mL
1	onion, minced	1
4	cloves garlic, minced	4
3	beets, peeled and ends cut flat	3
2	potatoes, peeled and ends cut flat	2
½ cup	chopped pepperoni	125 mL
1 tsp	dried parsley	5 mL
1 tsp	dried thyme	5 mL
½ tsp	freshly ground black pepper	2 mL
Pinch	kosher salt (optional)	Pinch
	Sour cream (optional)	

1. In a large pot, bring rice and broth to a boil over high heat. Reduce heat and simmer for 25 minutes, until slightly tender.

2. Meanwhile, in a medium skillet, heat oil over medium heat. Add onions and cook, stirring, for 3 to 5 minutes or until softened. Add garlic and cook, stirring, for 1 minute or until fragrant but not browned. Remove from heat.

3. Using a spiralizer, cut beets and potatoes into thin strands.

4. Add onion mixture, beet and potato strands, pepperoni, parsley, thyme and pepper to the rice mixture. Simmer for 10 to 15 minutes or until vegetables and rice are tender. Season with salt (if using). Serve topped with a dollop of sour cream, if desired.

Veggie Linguine with Gorgonzola, Green Beans and Sage

I love that we can make a creamy linguine with vegetables instead of wheat pasta. Fresh herbs and gorgonzola make this dish delectable.

MAKES 4 SERVINGS

Tip

Choose russet potatoes that are straight and not too thick, as they will work better in your spiralizer.

1	bag (10 oz/300 g) frozen cut green beans	1
4	russet potatoes, peeled and ends cut flat	4
2 tsp	kosher salt	10 mL
2 tsp	chopped fresh sage	10 mL
6 oz	soft gorgonzola cheese	175 g
2 to 3 tbsp	butter, softened, divided	30 to 45 mL
¼ tsp	freshly ground black pepper (optional)	1 mL
4	fresh sage leaves (optional)	4

1. Cook green beans according to package directions. Set aside.

2. Using a spiralizer, cut potatoes into thin strands. Add to a large pot filled with water. Add salt and bring to a boil. Reduce heat and simmer for 7 to 9 minutes or until just softened. Add green beans and cook for 1 minute. Drain, reserving ½ cup (125 mL) water.

3. In a large serving bowl, combine chopped sage, cheese and 2 tbsp (30 mL) butter. Add bean mixture and toss until cheese melts and coats potato strands. If sauce is too thick, add the remaining butter and reserved water, 1 tbsp (15 mL) at a time. If desired, sprinkle with pepper and top with sage leaves.

Variations

Thyme, oregano and basil, or a combination, are nice alternatives to the sage.

Roquefort or a creamy blue cheese can be used instead of the gorgonzola. The key is to choose a creamy cheese that will melt readily when the bean mixture is added to it.

Italian Potato Spaghetti Pie

This hearty potato noodle casserole is a quick and easy all-in-one meal that is perfect for a weeknight family dinner.

MAKES 6 SERVINGS

Tips

When purchasing sausage, check the packaging to make sure it is gluten-free. The packaging may say "no gluten ingredients"; however, you will still want to check if it is either certified gluten-free or specifically says that it has been made and packaged in an area where gluten cross-contamination could not occur.

Choose sweet and russet potatoes that are straight and not too thick, as they will work better in your spiralizer.

▶ **Preheat oven to 350°F (180°C)**
▶ **9-inch (23 cm) deep dish glass pie plate, sprayed with nonstick cooking spray**

2	sweet potatoes, peeled and ends cut flat	2
2	russet potatoes, peeled and ends cut flat	2
1	large egg, beaten	1
¼ cup	freshly grated Parmesan cheese	60 mL
1 tbsp	butter, melted	15 mL
2 tsp	olive oil	10 mL
8 oz	Italian sausage (bulk or casings removed)	250 g
½ cup	chopped onion	125 mL
½ cup	chopped green bell pepper	125 mL
1	clove garlic, minced	1
1	can (8 oz/228 mL) tomato sauce	1
1 tsp	dried oregano	5 mL
1 cup	cottage cheese, drained	250 mL
½ cup	shredded mozzarella cheese	125 mL

1. Using a spiralizer, cut sweet and russet potatoes into thin strands. Place in a large bowl and stir in egg, Parmesan cheese and butter. Press potato mixture onto bottom and up sides of prepared pie plate.

2. In a medium skillet, heat oil over medium heat. Add sausage, onion, green pepper and garlic; cook, stirring and breaking sausage up with a spoon, for 5 to 7 minutes or until sausage is no longer pink and onion is tender. Drain off fat. Stir in tomato sauce and oregano; cook until heated through.

3. Spread cottage cheese evenly over the bottom and sides of the potato crust. Spread sausage mixture over cottage cheese. Sprinkle with mozzarella.

4. Bake in preheated oven for 20 to 25 minutes or until bubbling and heated through. Let cool for 5 minutes. Cut into wedges and serve.

One-Pot Tomato Basil Zucchini Pasta

Enjoy this pleasing rich tomato basil sauce over zucchini noodles for a weeknight dinner that is quick to make and easy to clean up.

**MAKES
6 SERVINGS**

Tips

Use any leftover basil leaves as a garnish.

If you want to use prepared minced garlic, use 1½ tsp (7 mL).

For a vegetarian version of this recipe, use ready-to-use vegetable broth in place of the chicken broth.

3	cloves garlic, minced	3
1	small onion, sliced	1
⅓ cup	firmly packed fresh basil leaves, coarsely chopped	75 mL
2 tsp	dried oregano	10 mL
2 tsp	kosher salt	10 mL
¼ tsp	hot pepper flakes (optional)	1 mL
1	can (28 oz/796 mL) diced tomatoes, with juice	1
1½ cups	ready-to-use chicken broth	375 mL
1 tbsp	olive oil	15 mL
6	zucchini, ends cut flat	6
	Freshly grated Parmesan cheese	

1. In a Dutch oven, combine garlic, onion, basil, oregano, salt, hot pepper flakes (if using), tomatoes, broth and oil. Bring to a boil. Reduce heat and simmer for 5 minutes.

2. Meanwhile, using a spiralizer, cut zucchini into medium strands. Add to sauce and simmer, stirring gently, for 3 to 5 minutes or until cooked to desired tenderness. Serve sprinkled with cheese.

Squash Noodle and Mushroom Bake

The aroma of sautéing shallots, thyme, garlic and mushrooms will have you eager to get this dish assembled and out of the oven.

MAKES 4 SERVINGS

Variations

A combination of mushrooms, such as shiitake mushroom caps and white button mushrooms, can be used instead of the cremini.

You can use 1 tsp (5 mL) dried thyme in place of fresh.

▸ **Preheat oven to 375°F (190°C)**

▸ **8-inch (20 cm) square shallow baking dish, lightly sprayed with nonstick cooking spray**

2	butternut squash necks (at least 4 inches/10 cm long)	2
3 tbsp	butter	45 mL
¼ cup	sliced shallots	60 mL
3	cloves garlic, minced	3
12 oz	cremini mushrooms, sliced	375 g
1 tbsp	chopped fresh thyme	15 mL
½ tsp	kosher salt	2 mL
¼ tsp	freshly ground black pepper	1 mL
2 tbsp	cornstarch	30 mL
2 cups	whole milk	500 mL
1 cup	shredded Asiago cheese, divided	250 mL
	Fresh thyme sprigs (optional)	

1. Peel butternut squash necks and trim to 4 inches (10 cm) long, with flat ends. Using a spiralizer, cut squash into wide ribbons. Set aside.

2. In a large skillet, melt butter over medium-high heat. Add shallots and cook, stirring, for 3 minutes. Add garlic, mushrooms, thyme, salt and pepper; cook, stirring, for 8 minutes or until mushrooms are tender.

3. Place cornstarch in a Dutch oven over medium-high heat. Gradually add milk, whisking constantly. Bring to a boil and cook for 1 minute or until slightly thickened. Remove from heat and stir in ½ cup (125 mL) cheese until blended. Add mushroom mixture and squash, tossing well to combine. Spoon into prepared baking dish and sprinkle with the remaining cheese.

4. Bake in preheated oven for 25 to 30 minutes or until cheese melts and begins to brown. Garnish with thyme sprigs, if using.

Turkish Baklava Salmon and Roasted Spiral Vegetables

Baklava as a main course — who would dream of denying themselves such a decadent treat? This Turkish-inspired salmon is coated in a sweet, slightly spicy and crunchy coating that brings a flash of flavors to your palate.

MAKES 4 SERVINGS

Tips

Brown rice cereal, gluten-free rice cakes or gluten-free pretzels are nice substitutes for the gluten-free bread crumbs. Pulse them in a blender or food processor to get the ideal consistency. If you use salted pretzels, do not add salt to the salmon.

Serve with lemon wedges on the side, if desired.

▸ **Preheat oven to 400°F (200°C)**

▸ **11- by 7-inch (28 by 18 cm) glass baking dish, sprayed with nonstick cooking spray**

¼ cup	dry gluten-free bread crumbs	60 mL
¼ cup	walnuts, finely chopped	60 mL
4 tsp	chopped fresh parsley	20 mL
¼ cup	butter, melted	60 mL
3 tbsp	whole-grain mustard	45 mL
1½ tbsp	liquid raw honey	22 mL
1 lb	salmon fillet, cut into 4 equal pieces	500 g
	Kosher salt	
	Freshly ground black pepper	
4	yellow-fleshed potatoes (such as Yukon Gold), ends cut flat	4
3 tbsp	crème fraîche	45 mL
1 tsp	prepared horseradish	5 mL

1. In a small bowl, combine bread crumbs, walnuts and parsley. In another small bowl, combine butter, mustard and honey.

2. Place salmon, skin side down, in prepared baking dish and season with salt and pepper. Brush salmon with butter mixture, then sprinkle with bread crumb mixture. Bake in preheated oven for 20 to 25 minutes or until salmon is opaque and flakes easily when tested with a fork.

3. Meanwhile, using a spiralizer, cut potatoes into thin strands.

4. In a medium skillet over medium heat, combine crème fraîche and horseradish. Add potatoes and cook, stirring, for 5 to 7 minutes or until cooked to desired tenderness.

5. Serve potatoes alongside salmon.

Parmesan-Crusted Tilapia with Sweet-and-Spicy Slaw

Parmesan and herbs add impact to the lean, mild taste of tilapia. Paired with the sweet and spicy slaw, the result is an eye-catching, flavorful meal.

Tips

When handling carrots, you will want to wear kitchen gloves so you don't discolor your hands.

Choose carrots that are as straight as you can find to make it easier to cut them in your spiralizer. Thicker carrots work best, but choose those that are just large, not overgrown. Older, overgrown carrots take on a woody flavor.

▷ **Preheat oven to 350°F (180°C)**

▷ **13- by 9-inch (33 by 23 cm) glass baking dish, buttered**

Sweet-and-Spicy Slaw

2	carrots, peeled and ends cut flat	2
1	tart green apple (such as Granny Smith or Pink Lady), cored	1
1	small head cabbage, outer leaves removed, cut in half and ends cut flat	1
2 tbsp	hot pepper flakes	30 mL
2 tsp	kosher salt	10 mL
2 tsp	dry mustard	10 mL
1/3 cup	cider vinegar	75 mL
1/4 cup	liquid honey	60 mL
3 tbsp	olive oil	45 mL
1 tsp	poppy seeds	5 mL

Fish

2 lbs	skinless tilapia fillets (see tip, opposite)	1 kg
2 tbsp	freshly squeezed lemon juice	30 mL
1/2 cup	freshly grated Parmesan cheese	125 mL
3 tbsp	finely chopped green onions	45 mL
1/4 tsp	seasoning salt	1 mL
1/4 tsp	dried basil	1 mL
Pinch	freshly ground black pepper	Pinch
1/4 cup	butter, softened	60 mL
3 tbsp	mayonnaise	45 mL

1. *Slaw:* Using a spiralizer, cut carrots, apple and cabbage into medium strands. Toss strands together in a large bowl.

Most varieties of cabbage with tightly packed leaves work well in the spiralizer. I have had the best results with red and green cabbage.

Any firm white fish will work well in this dish in place of tilapia. Try cod, perch or walleye, among others. Just make sure your fish isn't too rich or intensely flavored.

2. In a small bowl, whisk together hot pepper flakes, salt, mustard, vinegar and honey. Gradually pour in oil, whisking continuously. Add to carrot mixture, along with poppy seeds, and toss to coat. Let stand while you prepare the tilapia, to blend the flavors.

3. *Fish:* Place tilapia in prepared baking dish, without overlapping. Brush the tops with lemon juice. Bake in preheated oven for 15 to 20 minutes or until fish is just starting to flake.

4. Meanwhile, in a small bowl, combine cheese, green onions, seasoning salt, basil, pepper, butter and mayonnaise until well blended.

5. Spread cheese mixture over top of fish. Bake for 5 minutes or until golden brown. Serve with slaw.

Variation

Add $\frac{1}{4}$ cup (60 mL) dried cranberries to the slaw for tartness and color.

Not Your Mother's Tuna Noodle Casserole

This down-home casserole is a comforting cold-weather dish loaded with zucchini noodles for a healthy and hearty meal. If you want your kids to eat more vegetables and fish, this is the dish to start with.

MAKES 4 SERVINGS

Tips

If you are unfamiliar with guar gum, give it a try. It is used as a thickening agent or binder in gluten-free and other hypoallergenic recipes. It is typically sold in 8-oz (250 g) containers at health food stores or online. You need only a small amount in your recipes. Guar gum is a good substitute in recipes that typically require gluten to provide structure and binding power.

If you cannot find guar gum, you can use your preferred thickening agent (such as 1 tsp/5 mL arrowroot flour) in its place.

> **Preheat oven to 375°F (190°C)**

> **11- by 7-inch (28 by 18 cm) glass baking dish, greased**

4	zucchini, ends cut flat	4
1 tsp	olive oil	5 mL
1	stalk celery, chopped	1
1	clove garlic, minced	1
½ cup	finely chopped onion	125 mL
½ tsp	guar gum (see tip, at left)	2 mL
½ cup	whole milk	125 mL
2	cans (each 6 oz/170 g) tuna packed in olive oil, drained and flaked	2
1 cup	frozen peas	250 mL
½ cup	sour cream	125 mL
2 tsp	Dijon mustard	10 mL
½ tsp	dried thyme	2 mL
¼ tsp	kosher salt	1 mL
¼ tsp	freshly ground black pepper	1 mL
½ cup	shredded Monterey Jack cheese	125 mL

1. Using a spiralizer, cut zucchini into wide ribbons. Set aside.

2. In a small skillet, heat oil over medium heat. Add celery and cook, stirring, for 2 to 3 minutes or until tender-crisp. Add garlic and cook, stirring, for about 30 seconds or until fragrant. Add onion and cook, stirring, for 5 to 7 minutes or until translucent. Remove from heat.

Choose zucchini that are straight and fairly even in diameter. This will make it easier to spiral-cut them evenly.

3. In a large bowl, combine guar gum and milk to create a slurry. Add celery mixture, tuna, peas, sour cream, mustard, thyme, salt and pepper, mixing well. Add zucchini and toss to combine. Transfer to prepared baking dish and cover with foil.

4. Bake in preheated oven for 20 minutes or until bubbling around the edges. Uncover and sprinkle with cheese. Bake for 5 to 10 minutes or until cheese is melted.

Spanish Creamy Tuna Noodle Casserole

The rich and spicy-sweet flavor of piquillo peppers adds just the right amount of Spanish influence to this quick and easy classic tuna noodle dish.

Tips

Piquillo peppers have a sweet, smoky taste without heat. You can substitute roasted red peppers if you can't find piquillo peppers, but the dish will not have the same depth of flavor. Leftover piquillo peppers can be used in any recipe that calls for roasted red peppers. Or you can stuff them with a soft creamy cheese for an interesting appetizer.

Using authentic, full-flavored Parmigiano-Reggiano creates a complex, yet subtle tango of flavors. If you can't find it, you can use regular Parmesan.

▸ **Preheat oven to 450°F (230°C)**
▸ **9-inch (23 cm) square glass or ceramic baking dish**

4	yellow summer squash, ends cut flat	4
4 tbsp	butter, divided	60 mL
1	onion, finely chopped	1
1 tbsp	cornstarch	15 mL
3 cups	half-and-half (10%) cream	750 mL
1	can (6 oz/170 g) tuna packed in olive oil, drained and flaked	1
1	jar (7 oz/200 mL) roasted piquillo peppers, drained and sliced	1
1½ cups	frozen baby peas	375 mL
½ cup	freshly grated Parmigiano-Reggiano cheese (see tip, at left)	125 mL
Pinch	kosher salt	Pinch
Pinch	freshly ground black pepper	Pinch
½ cup	crushed gluten-free rice crackers (about 15 to 20 crackers)	125 mL

1. Using a spiralizer, cut squash into medium strands. Set aside.

2. In a large saucepan, melt 3 tbsp (45 mL) butter over medium-high heat. Add onion and cook, stirring, for 3 to 4 minutes or until softened. Add cornstarch and cook, stirring briskly, for 1 minute. Stir in cream and bring to a gentle boil. Stir in squash. Reduce heat and simmer, stirring occasionally, for 4 to 6 minutes or until sauce is thickened and squash is tender. Remove from heat and gently stir in tuna, piquillo peppers, peas, cheese, salt and pepper. Transfer to baking dish.

3. In a small skillet, melt the remaining butter. Add crackers and toss to combine. Sprinkle over casserole.

4. Bake in preheated oven for 10 minutes or until bubbling and golden brown.

Colorful Squash Spirals with Tuna, Olives and Capers

The only thing you will love more than eating delicata squash is preparing it — it's super-easy to work with and makes a beautiful presentation.

MAKES 4 SERVINGS

Tips

Choose delicata squash that are shorter in length. When you cut off the ends, use a long spoon to scoop out the seeds. Shorter squash will make this easier to do.

If your delicata squash has a thicker skin than you prefer, you can peel the skin before using. You can easily check the thickness of the skin once you have cut off the ends.

Butternut squash works well in this dish, but will taste slightly sweeter. Use the neck of 1 medium butternut squash, peeled and trimmed to 4 inches (10 cm) long before spiralizing. Reduce the simmering time to 7 to 10 minutes.

2	cloves garlic, minced	2
$2/3$ cup	freshly grated Parmesan cheese, divided	150 mL
$1/2$ cup	chopped fresh parsley	125 mL
$1/3$ cup	chopped drained kalamata olives	75 mL
2 tbsp	drained capers	30 mL
1 tbsp	chopped fresh basil	15 mL
$1/4$ tsp	kosher salt	1 mL
$1/4$ tsp	freshly ground black pepper	1 mL
	Grated zest of 1 lemon (optional)	
5 tbsp	freshly squeezed lemon juice, divided	75 mL
$1/4$ cup	olive oil	60 mL
2	cans (each 6 oz/170 g) tuna packed in olive oil, drained and broken into large chunks	2
3	delicata squash, ends cut flat and seeds removed (see tips, at left)	3
$1\frac{1}{2}$ cups	ready-to-use chicken broth	375 mL
1 cup	water	250 mL
2 tsp	red wine vinegar	10 mL

1. In a large bowl, combine garlic, $1/2$ cup (125 mL) cheese, parsley, olives, capers, basil, salt, pepper, lemon zest (if using), 4 tbsp (60 mL) lemon juice and oil. Add tuna and gently toss to coat. Set aside.

2. Using a spiralizer, cut squash into wide strands.

3. In a large skillet, heat broth, water, vinegar and the remaining lemon juice over medium heat. Add squash and simmer, stirring occasionally, for 12 to 18 minutes or until cooked to desired tenderness. Using tongs, transfer squash to tuna mixture and toss gently. Sprinkle with the remaining cheese. Serve at room temperature.

Crab and Asparagus with Vegetable Noodles

The slightly sweet and buttery taste of kohlrabi combined with succulent crabmeat is a feast for your palate.

Tips

If you have difficulty finding kohlrabi, use another firm root vegetable, such as parsnips or turnips. You will need 4 medium parsnips or 6 small turnips for this recipe.

Canned crabmeat comes in a few typical varieties: lump, white and pink. Lump crabmeat is from the claw and has the strongest flavor. White crabmeat is from the body and is flakier and milder in taste. Pink crabmeat is a combination of lump and white meat. Any of these will work in this recipe, so choose the type that best fits your budget and taste preferences.

4	kohlrabi, peeled and ends cut flat	4
2 tbsp	butter	30 mL
2 tbsp	olive oil	30 mL
4	cloves garlic, minced	4
1¼ cups	dry white wine	300 mL
1½ tbsp	freshly squeezed lemon juice	22 mL
12 oz	asparagus, trimmed and cut diagonally into 2-inch (5 cm) lengths	375 g
2	cans (each 6 oz/170 g) crabmeat, drained (see tip, at left)	2
½ cup	chopped fresh flat-leaf (Italian) parsley	125 mL
Pinch	salt (optional)	Pinch
Pinch	freshly ground black pepper (optional)	Pinch
Pinch	freshly grated Parmesan cheese (optional)	Pinch

1. Using a spiralizer, cut kohlrabi into thin strands. Set aside.

2. In a large skillet, heat butter and oil over medium heat. Add garlic and cook, stirring, until fragrant. Stir in wine and lemon juice; simmer for about 10 minutes or until liquid is reduced by half.

3. Stir in kohlrabi and asparagus, cover and steam for 5 to 7 minutes or until asparagus is just tender-crisp and kohlrabi is just tender. Add crabmeat and cook, tossing gently, until heated through. Add parsley and season with salt and pepper (if using). Toss again. Transfer to a warm serving bowl and sprinkle with cheese, if desired.

Lemon-Garlic Shrimp with Zucchini Noodles

Zucchini noodles offer up a lighter pairing with marinated shrimp than traditional pasta, but the flavor is just as inviting.

Tips

Perfectly cooked shrimp are firm, slightly pink and form the letter C. It is very easy to overcook shrimp, so watch them carefully. Unlike some foods that become more tender with additional cooking, overcooked shrimp are tough.

A spring test works well to determine if your shrimp are properly done: hold the head end and pull the tail down. If the shrimp is cooked correctly, the tail will spring back.

3	cloves garlic, minced	3
1 tbsp	minced fresh parsley	15 mL
	Grated zest and juice of 1/2 lemon	
1 1/2 tsp	olive oil	7 mL
Pinch	kosher salt	Pinch
Pinch	freshly ground black pepper	Pinch
2	zucchini, ends cut flat	2
1 tbsp	butter or virgin coconut oil (approx.)	15 mL
12 to 15	large shrimp, peeled and deveined	12 to 15
1 1/2 cups	packed baby spinach	375 mL
	Juice of 1/2 lemon (optional)	

1. In a small bowl, combine garlic, parsley, lemon zest, lemon juice, oil, salt and pepper. Let marinade stand for 20 to 30 minutes to blend the flavors.

2. Using a spiralizer, cut zucchini into thin strands. Set aside.

3. In a large skillet, heat butter over medium heat. Add shrimp and marinade; cook for 1 minute. Flip the shrimp and cook for 1 minute (see tips, at left). Using a slotted spoon, transfer shrimp to a plate and set aside.

4. Add zucchini to the skillet and add more butter, if needed. Cook, stirring, for 1 to 2 minutes or until slightly softened. Return shrimp to the pan and add spinach; cook, tossing, for 1 to 2 minutes or until shrimp are pink and opaque, zucchini is softened and spinach is wilted. Squeeze lemon juice from remaining lemon half over top, if desired.

Basil Cream Chicken with Zucchini Fettuccine

This simple yet decadent creamy chicken pasta is infused with basil, mushrooms and onions for a deep, rich flavor.

Tips

You can use boneless skinless chicken thighs in place of the chicken breasts.

You can replace the fresh mushrooms with a 14-oz (398 mL) can of sliced mushrooms, drained.

Spiralize the onions into thin strands and then mince them to make preparation easier.

5	zucchini, ends cut flat	5
3 tbsp	olive oil, divided	45 mL
1 lb	boneless skinless chicken breasts, cut into chunks	500 g
12 oz	mushrooms, sliced	375 g
1 cup	minced onion	250 mL
3 tbsp	butter	45 mL
1½ tbsp	cornstarch	22 mL
2 cups	ready-to-use chicken broth	500 mL
1 cup	heavy or whipping (35%) cream	250 mL
2 tbsp	minced fresh basil	30 mL
¼ tsp	freshly ground black pepper	1 mL
⅓ cup	freshly grated Parmesan cheese	75 mL

1. Using a spiralizer, cut zucchini into thin strands. Set aside.

2. In a skillet, heat 2 tbsp (30 mL) oil over medium-high heat. Add chicken, mushrooms and onion; cook, stirring, for 5 to 7 minutes or until chicken is no longer pink inside.

3. Meanwhile, in a large saucepan, melt butter over medium heat. Quickly whisk in cornstarch until blended. Add broth and cream. Stir in basil and pepper; cook until bubbling. Reduce heat and simmer, stirring, for 2 minutes. Stir in chicken mixture, remove from heat and keep warm.

4. Add the remaining oil to the skillet and increase heat to medium. Add zucchini and cook, tossing, for 2 to 3 minutes or until softened and moisture has evaporated.

5. Divide zucchini among 4 plates and top with chicken and cream sauce. Serve sprinkled with cheese.

Chicken Cordon Bleu Casserole with Yellow Squash Noodles

Cordon bleu means "blue ribbon" in French, and this dish has all the makings of a first-prize-winning dish. It is light but with a little naughty decadence.

MAKES 6 SERVINGS

Tips

Check to make sure any shredded or cubed Swiss cheese you buy is certified gluten-free or has been packaged in a facility where there is no gluten cross-contamination.

You can substitute nut butter or cream for the coconut cream. Check the packaging to be sure they have no added artificial ingredients, sugars or dairy. You may also want to try making your own nut butter.

▸ **Preheat oven to 425°F (220°C)**
▸ **11- by 7-inch (28 by 18 cm) glass baking dish, sprayed with nonstick cooking spray**

7	yellow summer squash, ends cut flat	7
2 tbsp	extra virgin olive oil	30 mL
1½ lbs	boneless skinless chicken breasts, cut into 1-inch (2.5 cm) cubes	750 g
8 oz	Swiss cheese, cubed or shredded	250 g
8 oz	cooked ham, diced	250 g
½ cup	ready-to-use chicken broth	125 mL
1½ tbsp	arrowroot	22 mL
1 cup	coconut cream	250 mL
½ cup	dry white wine	125 mL
6 tbsp	virgin coconut oil, melted	90 mL
1 tsp	dry mustard	5 mL

1. Using a spiralizer, cut squash into wide ribbons. Spread squash over bottom of prepared baking dish.

2. In a large skillet, heat oil over medium heat. Add chicken and cook, stirring, for 7 to 9 minutes or until no longer pink inside.

3. Transfer chicken to a large bowl and add cheese and ham, tossing to combine. Spread evenly over squash ribbons.

4. In a medium bowl, whisk together broth and arrowroot. Whisk in coconut cream, wine, coconut oil and mustard. Pour into baking dish and stir gently to coat ingredients.

5. Bake in preheated oven for 15 to 20 minutes or until bubbling. Let cool for 5 minutes to firm up before serving.

Creamy Cajun Chicken with Parsnip and Celery Root Pasta

Cajun cuisine originated with French settlers in Louisiana. Very rustic in nature, this dish makes use of local ingredients, particularly peppers, onions, garlic and celery. It's typically served with rice, but this version takes advantage of the spiralizer to create an updated classic.

**MAKES
2 SERVINGS**

Tips

Try this dish for a fun Mardi Gras party. It's easy to make a bigger batch for a larger group.

To make your own Cajun seasoning, combine equal parts freshly ground black pepper, garlic powder, onion powder, cayenne pepper and paprika.

1	parsnip, peeled and ends cut flat	1
1	small celery root, peeled and ends cut flat	1
8 oz	boneless skinless chicken breasts, cut into thin strips	250 g
2 tsp	Cajun seasoning	10 mL
2 tbsp	olive oil	30 mL
1	small green bell pepper, chopped	1
1	small onion, chopped	1
1	clove garlic, minced	1
1/4 tsp	dried basil	1 mL
Pinch	kosher salt	Pinch
Pinch	freshly ground black pepper	Pinch
1 cup	heavy or whipping (35%) cream	250 mL
1/4 cup	freshly grated Parmesan cheese (optional)	60 mL

1. Using a spiralizer, cut parsnip and celery root into thin strands. Set aside.

2. Place chicken and Cajun seasoning in a bowl and toss to coat.

3. In a large skillet, heat oil over medium heat. Add chicken and cook, stirring, for 3 to 5 minutes or until chicken is no longer pink inside. Transfer chicken to a plate and tent with foil to keep warm.

4. Add green pepper and onion to the skillet and cook, stirring, for 5 to 7 minutes or until softened. Stir in garlic, basil, salt, black pepper and cream; increase heat and bring to a gentle boil. Reduce heat to medium and stir in parsnip and celery root; simmer for 5 to 7 minutes or until vegetables are cooked to desired tenderness. During the last minute of cooking, return chicken to the sauce. Serve sprinkled with cheese, if desired.

Spicy Apple-Glazed Chicken and Rutabaga Noodles

Mouthwatering golden roasted chicken breasts are the crowning touch to the gently sautéed spiral-cut rutabaga noodles.

MAKES 4 SERVINGS

Tips

Boneless skinless chicken thighs can be substituted for the chicken breasts in this recipe.

You can change up this recipe by using different types of fruit butters. Apricot, peach or pear butter are delicious options to try.

▶ **Preheat oven to 375°F (190°C)**
▶ **Baking sheet, sprayed with nonstick cooking spray**

¼ cup	apple butter	60 mL
¼ cup	spicy brown mustard	60 mL
¼ tsp	kosher salt	1 mL
¼ tsp	freshly ground black pepper	1 mL
4	thin-sliced boneless skinless chicken breast cutlets (each about 4 oz/125 g)	4
1	small rutabaga, peeled and ends cut flat	1
2 tbsp	butter	30 mL
2 tsp	chopped fresh thyme	10 mL
2 tbsp	chopped green onions	30 mL

1. In a bowl, combine apple butter, mustard, salt and pepper. Place chicken on prepared baking sheet and baste tops with apple butter mixture. Bake in preheated oven for 10 to 15 minutes or until no longer pink inside.

2. Meanwhile, using a spiralizer, cut rutabaga into medium strands.

3. In a medium skillet, heat butter over medium heat. Add rutabaga and thyme; cook, stirring, for 5 to 7 minutes or until rutabagas are cooked to desired tenderness.

4. Divide rutabagas among 4 bowls. Cut cooked chicken breasts into 1-inch (2.5 cm) strips and arrange over rutabagas. Top with green onions.

Caribbean Chicken and Plantains with Mango Coconut Salsa

Inspired by the cuisine of Puerto Rico, this dish melds many of the local favorites, including chicken, plantains, coconut, mango and, of course, a little bit of heat.

MAKES 6 SERVINGS

Tips

If you want to reduce the heat of this recipe, remove all or some of the seeds from the jalapeño.

Choose large plantains that are green (unripened) and relatively straight. Green plantains are firmer and work better in the spiralizer. If the strands break into smaller strands, that is fine.

Mango Coconut Salsa

2	mangos, chopped	2
½ cup	unsweetened shredded coconut	125 mL
½ cup	finely chopped red bell pepper	125 mL
½ cup	thinly sliced green onions	125 mL
½ cup	chopped fresh cilantro	125 mL
2 tsp	minced jalapeño pepper	10 mL
Pinch	kosher salt	Pinch
2 tbsp	freshly squeezed lime juice	30 mL

Spice Rub

1 tbsp	packed brown sugar	15 mL
2 tsp	ground cumin	10 mL
2 tsp	garlic powder	10 mL
2 tsp	dry mustard	10 mL
2 tsp	ancho chile powder	10 mL
2 tsp	paprika	10 mL
1 tsp	ground coriander	5 mL
Pinch	kosher salt	Pinch

Plantains

5	unripe plantains, peeled and ends cut flat	5
8 oz	thick-cut sliced bacon, cut into 1-inch (2.5 cm) pieces	250 g
2 tbsp	sesame oil (approx.)	30 mL
1 tbsp	chopped garlic	15 mL
Pinch	freshly ground black pepper	Pinch

Chicken

1½ lbs	boneless skinless chicken breasts, cut into 1½-inch (4 cm) cubes	750 g
2 tbsp	virgin coconut oil	30 mL
1½ tbsp	chopped garlic	22 mL
4 cups	ready-to-use chicken broth	1 L

The spice rub can be made ahead. Increase the quantity so you have more on hand to go with other dishes. Store this mixture in an airtight container in the refrigerator for up to 3 weeks.

1. *Salsa:* In a large bowl, combine mangos, coconut, red pepper, green onions, cilantro, jalapeño, salt and lime juice. Cover and refrigerate for at least 1 hour, until chilled, or for up to 2 days.

2. *Spice Rub:* In a large sealable plastic bag, combine brown sugar, cumin, garlic powder, mustard, ancho chile powder, paprika, coriander and salt. Seal and shake to combine. Set aside.

3. *Plantains:* Using a spiralizer, cut plantains into medium strands. Set aside.

4. In a large skillet, cook bacon over medium heat, stirring, until crisp. Transfer bacon to a plate lined with paper towels. Add enough sesame oil to the bacon grease to make 3 tbsp (45 mL) fat.

5. Add plantains and garlic to the fat in the skillet. Cook over medium heat, stirring gently, for 3 to 5 minutes or until plantains are golden brown. Remove from heat and stir in bacon and black pepper. Mash plantain mixture to a slightly coarse consistency. Keep warm.

6. *Chicken:* Add chicken to bag of spice rub, seal and shake to coat. In another large skillet, heat coconut oil over medium heat. Add garlic and cook, stirring, for 1 minute. Add chicken and cook, stirring, for 5 to 7 minutes or until no longer pink inside. Stir in broth and bring to a simmer. Reduce heat and simmer for 5 minutes or until broth is partially reduced.

7. Using an ice cream scoop or a large, deep spoon, scoop plantain mixture into a mound on each of six plates. Arrange chicken, with some of the broth, around plantain mounds. Pour more broth over plantains. Serve with salsa.

Raspberry-Chipotle Chicken with Cucumber Salad

The pairing of sweet raspberries and a bit of heat adds so much interest to these chicken breasts. Add a refreshing cucumber salad, and you have an exciting combination of flavors.

Tips

Chipotle chile peppers in adobo sauce typically come in 7-oz (198 mL) cans. Since you will be using only one pepper for this recipe, you will need to store the rest. Transfer them to a glass container and refrigerate for up to 1 month. They can also be frozen in small portions in ice cube trays and then individually wrapped and stored in the freezer. Use them in dips, salsas and soups. You can use just the chipotle pepper, for intense smoky heat; just the sauce, for a less hot sweet-and-sour flavor; or a combination of both.

Use seedless raspberry jam for the best results.

4	cucumbers, peeled and ends cut flat	4
1	small red onion, peeled and ends cut flat	1
	Kosher salt	
2	cloves garlic, minced	2
1	chipotle chile pepper in adobo sauce, finely chopped	1
2 tbsp	raspberry jam	30 mL
1½ tbsp	freshly squeezed lime juice	22 mL
1 tbsp	olive oil	15 mL
4	boneless skinless chicken breasts (about 1 lb/500 g total)	4
Pinch	freshly ground black pepper	Pinch
1 tbsp	granulated sugar	15 mL
2 tbsp	red wine vinegar	30 mL

1. Using a spiralizer, cut cucumbers into wide ribbons and pat dry. Cut onion into medium strands. Add both to a medium bowl and toss with 2 tsp (10 mL) salt. Set aside.

2. In a small saucepan, combine garlic, chipotle pepper, jam and lime juice; bring to a simmer over medium heat. Reduce heat and simmer, stirring frequently, for 4 to 5 minutes or until reduced to a syrup.

3. In a large skillet, heat oil over medium-high heat. Season chicken with pepper and a pinch of salt. Add to skillet and cook for 2 to 3 minutes per side or until no longer pink inside and a thermometer inserted in the thickest part of a breast registers 165°F (74°C). Spoon raspberry-chipotle syrup over chicken. Remove from heat and keep warm.

4. Combine sugar and vinegar. Drain any excess liquid from cucumber mixture. Add vinegar mixture and toss to coat. Serve with chicken.

Chicken and Tangy Peanut Sauce over Squash and Carrot Noodles

A very colorful combination of vegetables delivers an inviting foundation for the chicken and tangy peanut sauce.

Tips

The peanut sauce also makes a terrific dip for fresh peas in the pod, or a flavorful spread for sandwiches.

If desired, you can toast the sesame seeds in a small skillet over medium-high heat for 3 to 4 minutes or until fragrant.

1 tsp	minced gingerroot	5 mL
1 tsp	minced garlic	5 mL
½ tsp	granulated sugar	2 mL
½ cup	smooth peanut butter	125 mL
3 tbsp	rice vinegar	45 mL
1 tbsp	gluten-free soy sauce or tamari	15 mL
2 tsp	sesame oil	10 mL
⅓ to ½ cup	water	75 to 125 mL
3	zucchini, ends cut flat	3
3	yellow summer squash, ends cut flat	3
2	large carrots, peeled and ends cut flat	2
	Ice cold water	
4 cups	diced cooked chicken	1 L
¼ cup	chopped fresh cilantro	60 mL
2 tbsp	sesame seeds	30 mL

1. In a medium bowl, combine ginger, garlic, sugar, peanut butter, vinegar, soy sauce and oil until well blended. Gradually stir in water to reach desired consistency. (The squash strands will add liquid, so you may want to make the dressing slightly thicker than usual.)

2. Bring a pot of water to a boil over high heat. Meanwhile, using a spiralizer, cut zucchini, squash and carrots into thin strands, keeping the carrots separate. Add carrots to the boiling water and boil for 3 to 5 minutes or until cooked to desired tenderness. Using a slotted spoon, immediately transfer carrots to a bowl of ice cold water. Blanch zucchini and squash in the same way, but boil for 2 to 3 minutes. Drain the cooled vegetables thoroughly and pat dry if necessary.

3. Transfer blanched vegetables to a serving bowl. Top with chicken and drizzle with dressing. Sprinkle cilantro and sesame seeds on top.

Chicken Zucchini Tetrazzini

Chicken tetrazzini has been a favorite of mine since childhood and continues to be a favorite for my daughter and me. I love that I can now make it with fewer carbohydrates and calories.

MAKES 4 TO 6 SERVINGS

Tips

To cut down on preparation time, use a rotisserie chicken from your local grocery store. Shred enough chicken to make 1½ cups (375 mL). Skip step 2 and add the chicken in step 3, simmering it long enough to heat through.

A 4-oz (114 mL) can of mushroom stems and pieces, drained, can be used instead of the fresh mushrooms.

▸ **Preheat oven to 375°F (190°C)**
▸ **13- by 9-inch (33 by 23 cm) glass baking dish, greased**

8	zucchini, ends cut flat	8
¼ cup	butter, divided	60 mL
1 lb	boneless skinless chicken breasts	500 g
1 tbsp	kosher salt	15 mL
1 tbsp	freshly ground black pepper	15 mL
2 cups	sliced mushrooms	500 mL
½ cup	finely chopped onion	125 mL
2	cloves garlic, minced	2
1 tbsp	chopped fresh thyme	15 mL
½ cup	white wine or ready-to-use chicken broth	125 mL
⅓ cup	heavy or whipping (35%) cream	75 mL
2 cups	frozen peas (about 10 oz/300 g)	500 mL
	Chopped fresh parsley	

1. Using a spiralizer, cut the zucchini into thin strands. Set aside.

2. In a large skillet, melt half the butter over medium-high heat. Season chicken with salt and pepper, add to pan and reduce heat to medium. Cook for 8 to 12 minutes, turning occasionally, until chicken is no longer pink inside and a thermometer inserted in the thickest part of a breast registers 165°F (74°C). Remove chicken from the pan and cut into 1-inch (2.5 cm) cubes.

3. Add the remaining butter to the drippings in the skillet. Stir in mushrooms, onion, garlic, thyme, wine and cream; bring to a simmer. Reduce heat and simmer for about 5 minutes or until sauce is thickened. Stir in peas. Remove from heat and return chicken to the pan. Gently stir in zucchini. Pour into prepared baking dish.

4. Bake in preheated oven for 25 to 30 minutes or until bubbling. Let cool slightly for ease in cutting.

Chicken, Spiral Sweet Potato and Brie Pie

A quick and easy tart filled with chicken and sweet potatoes and pulled together with creamy, flavorful Brie delivers savory flavors in an elegant package.

	MAKES 4 SERVINGS	

Tips

Store-bought rotisserie chicken makes this dish a snap to prepare. A typical whole chicken yields about 3 cups (750 mL) of shredded chicken. Use 2 cups (500 mL) for this recipe and save the rest for another use. Leftover rotisserie chicken can be stored in the refrigerator for up to 3 days or in the freezer for up to 3 months.

If you like, you can toast the walnuts. Spread them on a rimmed baking sheet and toast in a 350°F (180°C) oven for 5 to 8 minutes, tossing once partway through, until fragrant but not darkened.

▶ **Preheat oven to 475°F (240°C), with rack in middle position**
▶ **Baking sheet, lined with parchment paper**

6 oz	firm Brie (with rind), divided	175 g
2	sweet potatoes, peeled and ends cut flat	2
2 cups	shredded rotisserie chicken (see tip, at left)	500 mL
1/4 cup	chopped walnuts	60 mL
1/4 tsp	kosher salt	1 mL
1/8 tsp	freshly ground black pepper	0.5 mL
1/4 cup	ready-to-use chicken broth	60 mL
1	9-inch (23 cm) gluten-free pie pastry round	1

1. Cut 4 oz (125 g) Brie into 1-inch (2.5 cm) pieces, including rind. Remove the rind from the remaining Brie and finely chop the cheese.

2. Using a spiralizer, cut sweet potato into medium strands.

3. In a large microwave-safe bowl, combine finely chopped Brie, sweet potato, chicken, walnuts, salt, pepper and broth. Cover and microwave on High for 1 to 2 minutes or until heated through. Remove from microwave and stir.

4. Place pie pastry round in center of prepared baking sheet. Spread chicken mixture evenly over dough, leaving a 1 1/2-inch (4 cm) border uncovered. Fold edge of dough over filling, pleating it every 2 to 3 inches (5 to 7.5 cm). Place Brie pieces on top, with rind facing up.

5. Bake in preheated oven for about 15 minutes, rotating the baking sheet halfway through, until crust is golden and cheese is melted. Let cool slightly before cutting and serving.

Chicken Tikka Masala over Potato Noodles

Infused with spices and inspiration from India, this tender chicken dish is creamy and deeply flavored. While the heart and soul of this dish remain the same, this version is served with twisty potato noodles instead of rice.

Tips

Choose russet potatoes that are not too thick, as they will work better in your spiralizer.

For more heat, add hot pepper flakes or cayenne pepper to the sauce in step 3. Start with ¼ tsp (1 mL) and taste before adding more.

2	cloves garlic, grated	2
½ tsp	kosher salt	2 mL
1 cup	plain yogurt	250 mL
3 tbsp	peanut oil, divided	45 mL
2 tbsp	freshly squeezed lemon juice	30 mL
1½ lbs	boneless skinless chicken breasts, cut into 1½-inch (4 cm) cubes	750 g
1 tbsp	finely grated gingerroot	15 mL
3 tbsp	garam masala	45 mL
2 tsp	ground coriander	10 mL
1½ tsp	ground cumin	7 mL
1 tbsp	butter	15 mL
1	small onion, thinly sliced	1
1	can (15 oz/425 mL) tomato purée	1
1 cup	heavy or whipping (35%) cream	250 mL
½ cup	water	125 mL
4	large russet potatoes	4
½ cup	chopped fresh cilantro	125 mL

1. In a large bowl, combine garlic, salt, yogurt, 1 tbsp (15 mL) peanut oil and lemon juice. Pierce chicken cubes with a fork. Add to the marinade and rub marinade into chicken. Cover and refrigerate.

2. In a small bowl, combine ginger, garam masala, coriander and cumin.

3. In a large saucepan, melt butter over medium-high heat. Add onion and cook, stirring, for 5 to 7 minutes or until lightly browned. Reduce heat to medium and stir in spice mixture, tomato purée, cream and water; bring to a boil. Reduce heat and simmer for 10 to 12 minutes or until slightly thickened.

Tip

The chicken tikka masala can be made ahead and refrigerated in an airtight container for up to 3 days. Prepare the potato noodles while you are reheating the sauce and right before serving.

4. Meanwhile, in a large skillet, heat 1 tbsp (15 mL) peanut oil over medium-high heat. Remove chicken from marinade, discarding marinade, and cook, stirring, for 1 to 2 minutes or until browned on all sides. Transfer chicken to sauce and simmer, stirring, for 5 to 7 minutes or until chicken is no longer pink inside. Turn off heat.

5. Peel potatoes and cut the ends flat. Using a spiralizer, cut potatoes into thin strands.

6. In the same skillet, heat the remaining peanut oil over medium heat. Add potatoes and cook, stirring, for 6 to 8 minutes or until softened. Transfer to a serving dish.

7. Top potatoes with cooked chicken mixture. Garnish with cilantro.

Chicken, Arugula and Spiral Radish Pizza

The cauliflower pizza crust in this recipe will surprise and delight even the serious pizza lover, and your kids will love to help you make it. Enjoy this recipe as is, or get creative with your own choice of toppings.

Tips

A 2-lb (1 kg) whole chicken yields about 2 cups (500 mL) shredded white meat and 1 cup (250 mL) dark meat.

Pick up your rotisserie chicken as the last item in your grocery cart so it stays hot (140°F/60°C). Use it within 2 hours of purchase or refrigerate.

▸ **Preheat oven to 425°F (220°C)**
▸ **Food processor or blender**
▸ **Colander, lined with cheesecloth, or nut milk bag**
▸ **Baking sheet, lined with parchment paper**

Pizza Crust

1½ lbs	cauliflower florets	750 g
2 tsp	ground flax seeds (flaxseed meal)	10 mL
⅓ cup	crumbled goat cheese	75 mL
1 tsp	minced garlic	5 mL
½ tsp	dried basil	2 mL
½ tsp	dried oregano	2 mL
¼ tsp	kosher salt	1 mL

Toppings

2 tbsp	extra virgin olive oil, divided	30 mL
1½ cups	shredded cooked chicken (preferably rotisserie)	375 mL
⅓ cup	ricotta cheese	75 mL
½ tsp	freshly ground black pepper	2 mL
½ tsp	hot pepper flakes	2 mL
3	large red radishes, ends cut flat	3
2 tbsp	white vinegar	30 mL
1 tsp	Dijon mustard	5 mL
1½ cups	packed baby arugula	375 mL

1. *Crust:* In food processor, pulse cauliflower until it resembles damp grains. You should have about 2 cups (500 mL).

Radishes come in an array of colors, shapes, sizes and flavors. While this recipe calls for red radishes, you can choose other varieties — just choose large radishes that are carrot-shaped for best results, otherwise they will not work in your spiralizer.

2. Transfer cauliflower to a microwave-safe bowl, cover, leaving a small opening to allow steam to escape, and microwave on High for 4 minutes. Carefully pour cauliflower into prepared colander and let drain and cool. Twist the cheesecloth to squeeze out as much liquid as possible, reserving 3 tbsp (45 mL) liquid. Add flax seeds to reserved liquid and mix well.

3. Return cauliflower to the bowl and stir in flax mixture, goat cheese, garlic, basil, oregano and salt until well blended. Shape into a ball.

4. On prepared baking sheet, press cauliflower ball out into a 1/4-inch (0.5 cm) thick circle. Bake in preheated oven for 12 to 15 minutes or until golden brown.

5. *Toppings:* Brush crust with 1 tbsp (15 mL) oil. Distribute chicken and ricotta evenly over crust. Sprinkle with black pepper and hot pepper flakes. Bake for 6 to 8 minutes or until cheese is melted and bubbly.

6. Meanwhile, using a spiralizer, cut radishes into wide ribbons.

7. In a medium bowl, whisk together vinegar, the remaining oil and mustard. Add radishes and arugula, tossing to coat.

8. Arrange arugula mixture on top of pizza. Cut into wedges and serve.

Variations

If you don't want to take the time to make the cauliflower crust, you can substitute a gluten-free pizza crust and bake according to package directions.

Add sliced black or green olives, to your liking, with the radishes in step 7.

BBQ Pork and Spiral Radish Pizza: Shredded barbecued pork is a terrific alternative to the chicken. If you have a leftover pork roast, shred the pork and mix it with your favorite gluten-free barbecue sauce.

Chicken Tostadas

Great for enjoying with friends and family during a football game, these tostadas are a crowd-pleaser, packed with flavor and ready in no time.

**MAKES
8 SERVINGS**

Tips

A 2-lb (1 kg) whole rotisserie chicken yields about 2 cups (500 mL) shredded white meat and 1 cup (250 mL) dark meat.

Pick up your rotisserie chicken as the last item in your grocery cart so it stays hot (140°F/60°C). Use it within 2 hours of purchase or refrigerate.

Instead of using a rotisserie chicken, you can roast your own chicken or use leftover chicken or turkey, shredded to yield 3 cups (750 mL).

For a festive meal or halftime party, serve with margaritas, chips, salsa and queso.

▶ **Preheat oven to 400°F (200°C)**
▶ **Baking sheets**

8	6-inch (15 cm) gluten-free corn tortillas	8
2 tbsp	olive oil	30 mL
3 cups	shredded rotisserie chicken (see tips, at left)	750 mL
½ cup	chopped fresh cilantro, divided	125 mL
2 cups	medium picante sauce	500 mL
1	can (16 oz/454 mL) refried beans	1
6	large red radishes, ends cut flat	6
1	large jicama, peeled and ends cut flat	1
½	onion, chopped	½
3 cups	shredded iceberg lettuce	750 mL
½ cup	sour cream	125 mL
¼ cup	crumbled queso añejo or Romano cheese	60 mL

1. Brush both sides of tortillas lightly with oil. Place in a single layer on baking sheets. Bake in preheated oven for 5 minutes. Turn tortillas and bake for 3 to 6 minutes or until crisp and light brown. Transfer to plates.

2. In a large saucepan, combine chicken, half the cilantro and picante sauce. Heat over medium heat, stirring, until warmed through.

3. Meanwhile, in a small saucepan, heat refried beans over medium-low heat, stirring, until warmed through.

4. Using a spiralizer, cut radishes and jicama into thin strands. Pat jicama strands dry.

5. In a large bowl, toss together radishes, jicama, onion, lettuce and the remaining cilantro.

6. Spread refried beans on top of each tortilla, then top with chicken mixture and a dollop of sour cream. Mound lettuce mixture on top and sprinkle with queso añejo.

Chicken-Apple Sausages with Autumn Vegetables

This hearty Austrian-inspired dish is bursting with flavor and texture. You may find that it becomes one of your go-to comfort foods.

MAKES 4 SERVINGS

Tips

At first glance, rutabagas may seem difficult to use, but once you get the hang of preparing them, you will find their earthy but simple taste is well worth the effort. For easy preparation, use a vegetable peeler or paring knife to remove the outer skin. Rutabagas often have a wax coating to preserve them during handling. Make sure to remove all of the wax.

When purchasing sausage, check the packaging to make sure it is gluten-free. The packaging may say "no gluten ingredients"; however, you will still want to check if it is either certified gluten-free or specifically says that it has been made and packaged in an area where gluten cross-contamination could not occur.

1 tbsp	butter	15 mL
3 tsp	olive oil, divided	15 mL
2	red onions, halved and thinly sliced	2
2	large heads Treviso radicchio, cored and thinly sliced	2
3 tbsp	balsamic vinegar	45 mL
Pinch	salt (optional)	Pinch
Pinch	freshly ground black pepper (optional)	Pinch
3	rutabagas, peeled and ends cut flat	3
4	cooked gluten-free chicken-apple sausages (each 3 oz/90 g)	4

1. In a heavy skillet, heat butter and 1 tsp (5 mL) olive oil over medium heat. Add onions and cook, stirring, for 15 to 20 minutes or until golden brown. Add radicchio and cook, stirring, for 2 minutes or until wilted. Add vinegar, increase heat to medium-high and cook for 1 to 2 minutes or until liquid is absorbed. Season with salt and pepper (if using).

2. Meanwhile, using a spiralizer, cut rutabagas into thin strands.

3. In a large skillet, heat the remaining oil over medium-high heat. Add rutabagas and cook, stirring, for 2 to 3 minutes. Push rutabagas to one side of the skillet. To the other side, add sausages and cook, turning often, for 5 to 7 minutes or until sausages are well browned and heated through and rutabagas are tender.

4. Serve sausages alongside rutabagas and radicchio mixture.

Savory Skillet Turkey Sausage with Potato and Celery Root Noodles

Onions, colorful peppers and garlic elevate the flavor of the sausage and potatoes in this delectable dish.

MAKES 4 SERVINGS

Tip

Use a paring knife to peel the skin off the celery root. You want to cut down to the creamy white flesh, removing the skin and darker internal layer. Depending on the size or awkward shape of your celery root, you may want to cut the root in half. Keep in mind that it needs to fit in your spiralizer.

	Nonstick cooking spray	
14 oz	smoked gluten-free turkey sausages (see tip, page 63)	420 g
1 tbsp	butter	15 mL
1 tbsp	olive oil	15 mL
1 cup	chopped onion	250 mL
1 cup	chopped red bell pepper	250 mL
1 cup	chopped green bell pepper	250 mL
1½ cups	frozen corn kernels, thawed	375 mL
4	russet potatoes, peeled and ends cut flat	4
1	small celery root, peeled and ends cut flat	1
1	clove garlic, minced	1

1. Coat a large skillet or cast-iron pan with cooking spray. Heat pan over medium-high heat. Add sausages and cook, turning often, for 2 to 3 minutes or until browned on all sides. Transfer sausages to a plate and slice diagonally.

2. Add butter and olive oil to the skillet and reduce heat to medium. Add onion, red pepper and green pepper; cook, stirring, for 5 to 7 minutes or until softened and starting to brown. Return sausages to the pan, add corn and cook, stirring, for 4 to 6 minutes or until heated through.

3. Meanwhile, using a spiralizer, cut potatoes and celery root into thin strands. Coat a medium skillet with cooking spray and heat over medium heat. Add potatoes, celery root and garlic; cook, stirring, for 6 to 8 minutes or until cooked to desired tenderness.

4. Divide potato mixture among 4 plates and top with sausage mixture.

Sausage with Zesty Tomato Cream Sauce and Parsnip Noodles

Sweet Italian sausage with a zesty tomato sauce will have you singing "Mamma Mia," and the parsnip noodles may even make you feel light enough to dance.

Tip

When purchasing sausage, check the packaging to make sure it is gluten-free. The packaging may say "no gluten ingredients"; however, you will still want to check if it is either certified gluten-free or specifically says that it has been made and packaged in an area where gluten cross-contamination could not occur.

1 tbsp	olive oil	15 mL
8 oz	gluten-free sweet Italian sausage (bulk or casings removed)	250 g
2	cloves garlic, minced	2
¼ cup	finely chopped onion	60 mL
¼ tsp	hot pepper flakes	1 mL
1	can (14 oz/398 mL) diced tomatoes, with juice	1
¾ cup	heavy or whipping (35%) cream	175 mL
¼ tsp	kosher salt	1 mL
4	parsnips, peeled and ends cut flat	4
¼ cup	freshly grated Parmesan cheese	60 mL
1½ tbsp	minced fresh parsley	22 mL

1. In a heavy skillet, heat oil over medium heat. Add sausage and cook, breaking it up with a spoon, for 7 to 9 minutes or until no longer pink. Add garlic, onion and hot pepper flakes; cook for about 5 minutes or until onion is tender. Add tomatoes, cream and salt; bring to a simmer. Reduce heat and simmer, stirring, for 4 to 6 minutes or until slightly thickened.

2. Meanwhile, using a spiralizer, cut parsnips into thin strands. Add to sauce and simmer, stirring, for 5 to 7 minutes or until parsnips are tender but firm. Serve sprinkled with cheese and parsley.

Variation

Sausage links are a nice alternative here. Brown the whole sausage, then slice on the diagonal and finish cooking in the sauce.

Straw and Hay Squash Pasta

This classic favorite gets a makeover with butternut squash noodles.

Variations

This dish is just as good when prepared with pancetta, bacon or ham in place of the prosciutto. Pancetta and bacon need to be cooked first. In step 3, omit the olive oil and cook the pancetta or bacon before adding the onion, garlic and cream.

Chopped asparagus is a wonderful substitute for the peas in this dish.

▶ **Preheat oven to 400°F (200°C)**
▶ **Rimmed baking sheet, lined with parchment paper**

2 cups	frozen peas (about 10 oz/300 g)	500 mL
2	butternut squash necks (at least 4 inches/10 cm long)	2
2 tbsp	olive oil, divided	30 mL
3 tbsp	butter	45 mL
1	small onion, finely chopped	1
2 tsp	minced garlic	10 mL
2/3 cup	heavy or whipping (35%) cream	150 mL
4 oz	thinly sliced prosciutto, rolled up and cut into 1/4-inch (0.5 cm) wide strips	125 g
Pinch	kosher salt	Pinch
Pinch	freshly ground black pepper	Pinch
1/2 cup	freshly grated Parmesan cheese	125 mL

1. Cook peas according to package directions. Drain and set aside.
2. Peel butternut squash necks and trim to 4 inches (10 cm) long, with flat ends. Using a spiralizer, cut squash into medium strands. Place on prepared baking sheet. Drizzle with $1\frac{1}{2}$ tbsp (22 mL) oil and toss to coat. Bake in preheated oven for 7 to 8 minutes or until al dente.
3. In a large skillet, heat the remaining oil and the butter over medium heat. Add onion and cook, stirring, for 5 to 7 minutes or until softened. Add garlic and cook, stirring, for 1 minute or until fragrant. Add cream and simmer for 2 to 3 minutes or until slightly reduced. Stir in peas and prosciutto. Add squash and toss to combine. Season with salt and pepper. Add Parmesan and toss again. Serve immediately.

Winter Squash Carbonara with Pancetta and Sage

Butternut squash covered with a creamy sauce and topped with pancetta imbues this dish with comfort-food goodness.

Tip

The bulbous end of the butternut squash can be used in a variety of ways. Try roasting it or using it to make soup.

2	butternut squash necks (at least 4 inches/10 cm long)	2
2 tbsp	olive oil	30 mL
4 oz	pancetta, chopped	125 g
1 tbsp	finely chopped fresh sage	15 mL
2	cloves garlic, minced	2
1	small onion, chopped	1
Pinch	kosher salt	Pinch
Pinch	freshly ground black pepper	Pinch
1/2 cup	ready-to-use chicken broth	125 mL
1/2 cup	heavy or whipping (35%) cream	125 mL
1/4 cup	finely grated pecorino cheese	60 mL
1 1/2 oz	pecorino cheese, shaved	45 g

1. Peel butternut squash necks and trim to 4 inches (10 cm) long, with flat ends. Using a spiralizer, cut squash into thin strands. Set aside.

2. In a large skillet, heat oil over medium-high heat. Add pancetta, reduce heat to medium and cook, stirring, for 5 to 7 minutes or until crisp. Add sage and toss to coat. Using a slotted spoon, transfer pancetta and sage to a small bowl and set aside.

3. Add garlic and onion to the skillet. Season with salt and pepper. Cook, stirring, for 6 to 8 minutes or until onion is translucent. Add broth and cream; bring to a gentle boil. Add squash, reduce heat and simmer for 7 to 9 minutes or until slightly softened. Stir in grated pecorino. Serve immediately, topped with shaved pecorino and reserved pancetta and sage.

Variation

You can substitute 4 zucchini for the butternut squash, but the dish will not be as sweet and nutty-flavored. Because zucchini has a very high water content, you will want to reduce or eliminate the chicken broth, depending upon the desired consistency.

Pancetta and Lentils with Zucchini Pasta

Aromatic pancetta, onions and garlic in a lentil and tomato sauce provide rich flavor for the zucchini pasta.

Tip

To cut basil into chiffonade, remove stems and stack 10 or more leaves together. Roll the leaves lengthwise into a fairly tight spiral, then cut crosswise into thin strips. Fluff the strips.

6	zucchini, ends cut flat	6
3 tbsp	olive oil, divided	45 mL
4 oz	chopped pancetta	125 g
½ cup	finely chopped onion	125 mL
4	cloves garlic, minced	4
½ tsp	hot pepper flakes	2 mL
1	can (28 oz/796 mL) diced tomatoes, with juice	1
10	basil leaves, cut into chiffonade or roughly chopped, divided	10
	Kosher salt	
1 cup	ready-to-use reduced-sodium chicken broth (optional)	250 mL
1	can (14 oz/398 mL) French green (Puy) lentils, drained	1
½ cup	freshly grated Parmesan cheese, divided	125 mL
Pinch	freshly ground black pepper (optional)	Pinch

1. Using a spiralizer, cut zucchini into thin strands. Set aside.

2. In a large skillet, heat 2 tbsp (30 mL) oil over medium heat. Add pancetta and cook, stirring, for 5 to 7 minutes or until crisp. Add onion and cook, stirring, for about 2 minutes or until translucent. Add garlic and hot pepper flakes; cook, stirring, for about 2 minutes or until garlic begins to brown.

Tip

Dried French green
(Puy) lentils can be used
instead of canned. Cook
the lentils according to
packaged directions.

3. Stir in tomatoes, 8 chopped basil leaves and $\frac{1}{2}$ tsp
   (2 mL) salt; increase heat to medium-high and bring
   to a boil. Boil for 3 minutes. If desired, gradually add
   broth to thin the sauce to desired consistency. Reduce
   heat to medium-low and simmer, stirring occasionally,
   for 5 to 7 minutes or until slightly thickened.

4. Stir in zucchini and lentils; simmer for 3 to 4 minutes
   or until zucchini is cooked to desired tenderness.
   Remove from heat and add half the cheese. If
   desired, season with a pinch of salt and black pepper.
   Gently toss.

5. Divide zucchini mixture among 4 plates. Drizzle with
   the remaining oil and top with the remaining basil
   and cheese.

Pancetta, Chèvre and Candied Walnut Sweet Potato Pasta

The marriage of ingredients in this delicious dish delivers a pleasant savory taste you are sure to enjoy.

MAKES 4 SERVINGS

Tip

Choose sweet potatoes that are straight and not too thick, as they will work better in your spiralizer.

1 cup	walnut halves	250 mL
1/4 cup	granulated sugar	60 mL
1 tbsp	butter	15 mL
2	large sweet potatoes, peeled and ends cut flat	2
1 tbsp	olive oil	15 mL
1/2 tsp	kosher salt	2 mL
4 oz	finely chopped pancetta	125 g
1 cup	crumbled chèvre cheese, divided	250 mL
2 tbsp	water	30 mL

1. In a medium skillet, combine walnuts, granulated sugar and butter. Heat over medium heat, stirring constantly, for 5 minutes or until sugar is dissolved and nuts are coated. Remove from heat, transfer to a sheet of parchment paper and quickly separate the nuts. Let stand for 5 to 7 minutes or until coating hardens.

2. Meanwhile, using a spiralizer, cut sweet potatoes into thin strands.

3. In a large skillet, heat oil over medium heat. Add sweet potatoes and salt; cook, stirring, for 6 to 8 minutes or until sweet potatoes are softened. Transfer sweet potatoes to a plate and set aside.

4. Add pancetta to the skillet and cook, stirring, for 5 to 7 minutes or until crisp. Reduce heat to medium-low and add 1/2 cup (125 mL) cheese and water, stirring until cheese is melted. Add sweet potatoes and toss to combine. Serve warm, topped with the remaining cheese and candied walnuts.

Variation

Chèvre is a cheese made from goat's milk. You can substitute low-fat ricotta or feta cheese. Low-fat, soft, creamy cheeses will work best in this recipe.

BLT Squash Pasta

The flavors of the classic bacon, lettuce and tomato sandwich highlight this colorful pasta dish made with creamy, sweet butternut squash.

**MAKES
4 SERVINGS**

Tip

The bulbous end of the butternut squash contains seeds, so it does not spiralize well. Try roasting it instead, for a luscious side dish with any meal. Peel the squash, remove seeds and cut into 1½-inch (4 cm) cubes. Toss with melted butter, brown sugar, salt and pepper and roast in a 400°F (200°C) oven for 20 to 25 minutes.

2	butternut squash necks (at least 4 inches/10 cm long)	2
12 oz	thick-cut sliced bacon	375 g
2 cups	grape tomatoes, halved	500 mL
¼ tsp	kosher salt	1 mL
8 oz	baby spinach	250 g
¼ cup	grated Romano cheese	60 mL
½ tsp	freshly ground black pepper	2 mL

1. Peel butternut squash necks and trim to 4 inches (10 cm) long, with flat ends. Using a spiralizer, cut squash into medium strands. Set aside.

2. In a large skillet, cook bacon over medium heat for 6 to 8 minutes or until crisp. Transfer bacon to a plate lined with paper towels. Let cool, then crumble.

3. Drain off all but 2 tbsp (30 mL) bacon fat from the skillet. Add squash to the pan and cook, stirring, for 3 minutes. Add tomatoes and salt; cook, stirring, for 2 to 3 minutes. Add spinach and cook, stirring for 1 to 2 minutes or until spinach is just wilted and squash is just tender. Serve warm, sprinkled with bacon, cheese and pepper.

Variation

For a peppery flavor, replace the spinach with young arugula. Baby kale is another tasty alternative.

Sweet-and-Savory Gluten-Free Bread Pudding

We often think of bread pudding as a dessert, but give it some bacon, leeks and sweet potatoes with just a hint of apple and you have a savory, comforting main course.

**MAKES
8 SERVINGS**

Tip

Leeks are grown packed in sandy soil and retain this soil right into your kitchen. To clean them, cut the root ends and green tops off. Trim to 4-inch (10 cm) sections, then slice down the full length of the leek. Separate the sections and add to a large bowl filled with cold water. Using your fingers, rinse off any remaining dirt. The leeks will float and the dirt will fall to the bottom. Pat dry before slicing.

▶ **Preheat oven to 350°F (180°C)**
▶ **12-cup (3 L) glass baking dish, buttered**

12	slices gluten-free bread, cut into 1-inch (2.5 cm) cubes (about 6 cups/1.5 L)	12
6	sweet potatoes, peeled and ends cut flat	6
8 oz	sliced bacon	250 g
3	leeks (white and light green parts only), cut into thin slices	3
	Kosher salt	
Pinch	freshly ground black pepper	Pinch
¼ cup	unsweetened apple juice	60 mL
1 tbsp	chopped fresh thyme	15 mL
2	large eggs, lightly beaten	2
1¼ cups	whole milk	300 mL
1 cup	heavy or whipping (35%) cream	250 mL
½ cup	crumbled blue cheese (about 2 oz/60 g)	125 mL
½ cup	candied walnuts (store-bought or follow step 1, page 68)	125 mL

1. Place bread cubes on a baking sheet and bake in preheated oven for 15 minutes or until lightly toasted, tossing two to three times. Remove from oven, leaving oven on.

2. Meanwhile, using a spiralizer, cut sweet potatoes into thin strands. Set aside.

This dish can be prepared through step 5 and then covered and refrigerated for up to 2 days. Let stand at room temperature for 10 to 15 minutes before baking or add 10 to 12 minutes to the baking time.

3. In a large skillet, cook bacon over medium heat for 4 to 6 minutes or until crisp. Transfer bacon to a plate lined with paper towels. Let cool, then crumble.

4. Add leeks to the fat remaining in the skillet and cook, stirring, for 3 to 4 minutes or until lightly browned. Add sweet potatoes, a pinch of salt, pepper and apple juice; cook for 4 to 6 minutes or until sweet potatoes are slightly tender and juice is almost evaporated. Remove from heat and gently stir in toasted bread cubes, crumbled bacon and thyme. Spoon into prepared baking dish.

5. In a large bowl, whisk together eggs, milk, cream and 1 tsp (5 mL) salt. Pour over bread mixture, gently pressing bread down into the liquid so all pieces are covered. Let stand for 15 minutes.

6. Bake for 45 to 50 minutes or until puffed and golden. Serve sprinkled with blue cheese and candied walnuts.

Creamy Alfredo Vegetable Pasta with Prosciutto and Peas

You will want to dive right in to this lighter take on a classic, creamy Alfredo dish with an abundance of mouthwatering ingredients.

MAKES 4 SERVINGS

Tip

For convenience, you can use a 7-oz (200 mL) can of sliced mushrooms, drained, instead of the fresh mushrooms. Add them after the prosciutto has cooked for 5 to 7 minutes and is almost crisp.

4	zucchini, ends cut flat	4
2 tbsp	olive oil	30 mL
8 oz	mushrooms, sliced	250 g
2 oz	prosciutto, chopped	60 g
1½ cups	heavy or whipping (35%) cream	375 mL
⅓ cup	butter	75 mL
1 cup	freshly grated Parmesan cheese, divided	250 mL
Pinch	kosher salt (optional)	Pinch
Pinch	freshly ground white or black pepper	Pinch
Pinch	ground nutmeg	Pinch
1 cup	frozen peas, thawed	250 mL

1. Using a spiralizer, cut zucchini into thin strands. Set aside.

2. In a large skillet, heat oil over medium heat. Add mushrooms and prosciutto; cook, stirring, for 6 to 8 minutes or until mushrooms are softened and prosciutto is slightly crisp. Set aside.

3. In a medium saucepan, bring cream and butter to a gentle boil over medium-high heat. Reduce heat and simmer, stirring, for 3 to 5 minutes or until sauce begins to thicken. Whisk in ⅓ cup (75 mL) cheese and simmer, stirring, for 1 to 2 minutes or until creamy and smooth. Remove from heat and stir in 2 tbsp (30 mL) cheese, salt (if using), pepper and nutmeg.

4. Add zucchini, peas and cream sauce to the skillet, tossing gently. Return skillet to low heat and simmer, stirring, for 2 to 3 minutes or until zucchini is cooked to desired tenderness. Serve garnished with the remaining cheese.

Five-Spice Pork Lo Mein with a Twist

A combination of sautéed meat, vegetables and a savory five-spice sauce coalesce into a luscious dish that is ready in minutes.

Tip

Chinese five-spice powder is readily available in grocery stores. It is a blend of ground cinnamon, cloves, fennel seeds, star anise and Szechuan peppercorns. You can make your own by grinding equal amounts of these ingredients (or adjusting the proportions to your taste). Toasting the cloves, fennel seeds and peppercorns before grinding will give your spice blend a deeper, more complex flavor.

6	zucchini, ends cut flat	6
1 lb	pork tenderloin, trimmed and cut into thin strips	500 g
2 tsp	grated gingerroot	10 mL
1 tbsp	Chinese five-spice powder	15 mL
½ tsp	salt, divided	2 mL
2 tbsp	peanut oil	30 mL
¼ cup	hoisin sauce	60 mL
¼ cup	water (optional)	60 mL
½ cup	chopped green onions	125 mL

1. Using a spiralizer, cut zucchini into thin strands. Set aside on a paper towel to drain.

2. In a medium bowl, combine pork, ginger, five-spice powder and half the salt, tossing to coat.

3. In a large skillet, heat oil over medium-high heat. Add pork mixture and cook, stirring, for 3 to 5 minutes or until browned. Stir in hoisin sauce and the remaining salt. Add zucchini and cook, stirring, for 2 to 3 minutes or until just a hint of pink remains inside pork and zucchini is just tender. If desired, gradually add water to achieve the desired consistency. Remove from heat and add green onions, tossing well to combine. Serve immediately.

Curry Beef with Sweet Potato Noodles

A spicy beef curry adds a touch of pizazz to tender, velvety sweet potato noodles. The preparation is easy, and you can be attending to other things during much of this recipe's long cooking time.

Tip

Major Grey chutney has a sweet and tangy flavor courtesy of mangos, ginger, raisins, sugar and spices. It is common in both British and Indian cuisine. It's great as an accompaniment to Indian dishes or served with Cheddar cheese as an appetizer or snack. You can use another similar chutney, if desired.

3 tbsp	canola oil, divided (approx.)	45 mL
1 lb	boneless stewing beef, cut into 1-inch (2.5 cm) pieces	500 g
Pinch	freshly ground black pepper	Pinch
	Kosher salt	
1	large onion, sliced	1
2	cloves garlic, chopped	2
3	whole cloves	3
1	3-inch (7.5 cm) cinnamon stick	1
1	bay leaf	1
1/4 tsp	hot pepper flakes	1 mL
2	tomatoes, quartered	2
1 tbsp	minced gingerroot	15 mL
1 tbsp	curry powder	15 mL
3/4 cup	whole milk	175 mL
3 tbsp	Major Grey chutney	45 mL
1 1/2 tbsp	freshly squeezed lemon juice	22 mL
4	sweet potatoes, ends cut flat	4
3 tbsp	chopped fresh cilantro	45 mL

1. In a large heavy skillet, heat 1 tbsp (15 mL) oil over medium-high heat. Season beef with pepper and a pinch of salt. Working in batches, add beef to pan and cook, stirring, for 7 minutes or until browned on all sides, adding oil as necessary between batches. Using a slotted spoon, transfer beef to a plate.

Tip

Choose sweet potatoes that are straight and not too thick, as they will work better in your spiralizer.

2. Add 1 tbsp (15 mL) oil to the skillet and reduce heat to medium. Add onion and cook, stirring, for 5 to 7 minutes or until browned. Return beef to the pan and add garlic, cloves, cinnamon stick, bay leaf and hot pepper flakes; cook, stirring, for 1 minute. Stir in tomatoes, ginger, curry powder, $\frac{1}{2}$ tsp (2 mL) salt, milk, chutney and lemon juice; bring to a boil. Reduce heat to low, cover and simmer, stirring occasionally, for about 2 hours or until beef is tender. Uncover, increase heat to medium and cook for 5 to 7 minutes or until slightly thickened.

3. Meanwhile, using a spiralizer, cut sweet potatoes into medium strands. Add to the beef mixture, tossing gently, and cook, uncovered, for 5 to 7 minutes or until cooked to desired tenderness and sauce is slightly thickened. Discard cinnamon stick and bay leaf. Serve immediately, sprinkled with cilantro.

Mexican Squash Spaghetti Pie

Tender squash spaghetti forms a crust that's filled with beefy picante sauce, green chiles, black olives and loads of cheese.

Tips

Choose summer squash that are relatively straight and at least 1½ inches (4 cm) in diameter. They should not have any soft spots or bruising.

For a milder flavor, use 1 roasted green bell pepper, chopped, in place of the green chiles. For instructions on roasting peppers, see step 1, page 162

Variation

In place of the yellow summer squash, try 6 to 7 chayote squash, a native Mexican squash. You will need to pit them before spiralizing. The skin is edible, but many cooks choose to peel it off before use. Cook them as you would the summer squash.

▶ **Preheat oven to 350°F (180°C)**
▶ **9-inch (23 cm) deep-dish glass pie plate, greased**

1 lb	lean ground beef	500 g
1	can (4½ oz/127 mL) chopped green chiles	1
1	can (4½ oz/127 mL) sliced ripe olives, drained	1
2 cups	picante sauce	500 mL
5	yellow summer squash, ends cut flat	5
2 tsp	olive oil	10 mL
2 tsp	ground cumin	10 mL
1	large egg, beaten	1
⅓ cup	freshly grated Parmesan cheese	75 mL
1 tbsp	melted butter	15 mL
1 cup	ricotta cheese	250 mL
1 cup	shredded mozzarella cheese	250 mL

1. In a medium skillet, cook beef over medium-high heat, breaking it up with a spoon, for 7 to 9 minutes or until no longer pink. Drain off fat. Add chiles, olives and picante sauce; cook for 4 to 6 minutes or until bubbling. Remove from heat and set aside.

2. Using a spiralizer, cut squash into thin strands.

3. In a large skillet, heat oil over medium heat. Add squash and cook, stirring, for 3 to 5 minutes or until tender and liquid from squash has evaporated.

4. Transfer squash to a medium bowl and stir in cumin, egg, Parmesan and butter until well combined. Press squash mixture on the bottom and up the sides of prepared pie plate. Spread ricotta on top. Top with beef mixture.

5. Bake in preheated oven for 30 minutes or until bubbling. Sprinkle with mozzarella. Let stand for 5 minutes, then cut into wedges.

Roasted Beets and Carrots with Rosemary Garlic Butter

Ruby red beets and vibrant orange carrots coalesce with rosemary and garlic to create a side dish that is appealing in both color and taste.

MAKES 4 TO 6 SERVINGS

Tips

When handling beets and carrots, you will want to wear kitchen gloves so you don't discolor your hands.

Separating the beets from the carrots keeps the carrots from turning red or pink from the beet juice.

▸ **Preheat oven to 425°F (220°C), with one rack in the upper third and one in the bottom third**

▸ **2 rimmed baking sheets, lined with parchment paper**

3	carrots, peeled and ends cut flat	3
2	cloves garlic, minced, divided	2
2 tsp	kosher salt, divided	10 mL
½ tsp	freshly ground black pepper, divided	2 mL
½ tsp	dried rosemary, divided	2 mL
3 tbsp	butter, melted, divided	45 mL
4	red beets, scrubbed and ends cut flat	4

1. Using a spiralizer, cut carrots into medium strands. Place in a bowl and add half each of the garlic, salt, pepper, rosemary and butter. Toss to coat.

2. Using a spiralizer, cut beets into wide ribbons. Place in a separate bowl and add the remaining garlic, salt, pepper, rosemary and butter. Toss to coat.

3. Add the beets to one prepared baking sheet and the carrots to the other.

4. Place one baking sheet in the upper third of the preheated oven and the other in the bottom third. Bake for 5 minutes. Pull out baking sheets and turn vegetables. Return to the oven, swapping the sheets' positions on the racks. Bake for 5 minutes or until vegetables are browned and just tender. Let cool slightly, then toss together in a serving bowl.

Variation

Top with toasted pine nuts just before serving.

Curly Zucchini, Carrot and Celery Casserole

I kicked up the heat a notch with a touch of horseradish in this veggie casserole, which pairs well with a roasted beef or pork main dish.

MAKES 4 SERVINGS

Tip

Choose carrots that are as straight as you can find to make it easier to cut them in your spiralizer. Thicker carrots work best, but choose those that are just large, not overgrown. Older, overgrown carrots take on a woody flavor.

▶ **Preheat oven to 375°F (190°C)**

▶ **8-inch (20 cm) square shallow glass baking dish, lightly sprayed with nonstick cooking spray**

3	large carrots, peeled and ends cut flat	3
2	zucchini, ends cut flat	2
2 tbsp	sunflower oil	30 mL
1	stalk (rib) celery, chopped	1
¼ tsp	prepared horseradish	1 mL
¼ tsp	dried dillweed	1 mL
¼ tsp	kosher salt	1 mL
¼ tsp	freshly ground black pepper	1 mL
¼ cup	mayonnaise	60 mL
¼ cup	ready-to-use vegetable broth	60 mL
¼ cup	freshly grated Parmesan cheese	60 mL

1. Using a spiralizer, cut carrots and zucchini into wide ribbons, keeping them separate.

2. In a large skillet, heat oil over medium heat. Add celery and cook, stirring, for 2 to 3 minutes or until translucent. Add carrots and cook, stirring, for 4 to 5 minutes or until slightly softened. Add zucchini and cook, tossing gently, for 1 minute.

3. In a medium bowl, combine horseradish, dill, salt, pepper, mayonnaise and broth. Add zucchini mixture and gently toss to coat. Transfer to prepared baking dish.

4. Bake in preheated oven for 15 minutes. Sprinkle cheese on top. Bake for 5 minutes or until top is golden brown and edges are bubbling.

Braised Squash with Rosemary, Sage and Apple Cider Glaze

If you haven't tried delicata squash, you will be pleasantly surprised by its rich flavor, creamy texture and easy preparation. Rosemary, sage and apple cider merge to create a luscious glaze for the squash in this delectable and eye-catching side dish.

**MAKES
6 SERVINGS**

Tips

Choose delicata squash that are shorter in length. When you cut off the ends, use a long spoon to scoop out the seeds. Shorter squash will make this easier to do.

If your delicata squash has a thicker skin than you prefer, you can peel the skin before using. You can easily check the thickness of the skin once you have cut off the ends.

Butternut squash works well in this dish, but will taste slightly sweeter. Use the neck of 1 medium butternut squash, peeled and trimmed to 4 inches (10 cm) long before spiralizing. Reduce the simmering time to 7 to 10 minutes.

3	delicata squash, ends cut flat and seeds removed (see tips, at left)	3
3 tbsp	butter	45 mL
1/4 cup	coarsely chopped fresh sage	60 mL
1 tbsp	coarsely chopped fresh rosemary	15 mL
1/2 tsp	kosher salt	2 mL
1 1/2 cups	unsweetened apple cider	375 mL
1 cup	water	250 mL
2 tsp	red wine vinegar	10 mL
Pinch	freshly ground black pepper (optional)	Pinch

1. Using a spiralizer, cut squash into wide ribbons.
2. In a large skillet, melt butter over low heat. Add sage and rosemary; cook, stirring, for 2 to 3 minutes or until butter starts to turn golden brown. Add squash, salt, apple cider, water and vinegar; bring to a simmer over medium heat. Reduce heat and simmer, stirring occasionally, for 15 to 20 minutes or until cider has boiled down to a glaze and squash is tender. Season with pepper (if using). Serve warm.

Ginger-Glazed Roasted Squash

Rich fall flavors of squash, maple syrup and pecans come together in this comforting side dish with a hint of Southern charm.

**MAKES
4 SERVINGS**

Tip

Glazed pecans can be stored in an airtight container in the refrigerator for up to 2 weeks or in the freezer for up to 3 months. They are a perfect addition to a candy dish, either by themselves or mixed with other snacks. You can also add them to a decorative jar, tied with a ribbon or other decoration, for a personalized holiday gift.

▸ **Preheat oven to 400°F (200°C), with one rack in the upper third and one in the bottom third**

▸ **2 rimmed baking sheets, 1 lined with foil and 1 with parchment paper**

1 tbsp	butter	15 mL
1 tbsp	packed brown sugar	15 mL
1 tbsp	pure maple syrup	15 mL
1 cup	pecan halves	250 mL
3	butternut squash necks (at least 4 inches/10 cm long)	3
2 tsp	kosher salt	10 mL
1½ tsp	ground ginger	7 mL
2 tbsp	olive oil	30 mL

1. In a medium skillet, melt butter over medium heat. Add brown sugar and maple syrup; cook, stirring constantly, until bubbling. Add pecans and cook, stirring constantly, for 2 to 3 minutes or until well coated.

2. Spread pecan mixture on foil-lined baking sheet. Bake in preheated oven for 3 to 5 minutes or until golden brown. Transfer pecans to a plate, leaving oven on, and let cool completely, about 30 minutes. Replace the foil on the baking sheet with parchment paper.

3. Meanwhile, peel squash necks and trim to 4 inches (10 cm) long, with flat ends. Using a spiralizer, cut squash into wide ribbons. Place in a large bowl and add salt, ginger and oil, tossing well to coat. Transfer to prepared baking sheets, leaving space between each squash ribbon.

4. Place one baking sheet in the upper third of the preheated oven and the other in the bottom third. Bake for 5 minutes. Pull out baking sheets and turn squash. Return to the oven, swapping the sheets' positions on the racks. Bake for 5 minutes or until squash is browned and tender.

5. Chop ½ cup (125 mL) of the pecans. Transfer squash to a large bowl and toss with the chopped pecans and the remaining pecan halves. Serve immediately.

Crispy Baked Shoestring Sweet Potato Fries

Curly, crunchy sweet potato strings with a hint of seasoning will delight kids and adults alike. This recipe works beautifully as a side dish to any meal, but also makes a great snack.

MAKES 2 SERVINGS

Tip

Choose sweet potatoes that are straight and not too thick, as they will work better in your spiralizer.

▸ **Preheat oven to 400°F (200°C)**
▸ **Rimmed baking sheet, lined with parchment paper**

1	large sweet potato, peeled and ends cut flat	1
2 tbsp	olive oil	30 mL
1 tbsp	seasoning salt	15 mL

1. Using a spiralizer, cut sweet potato into thin strands. Place on prepared baking sheet. Drizzle oil over top and toss to coat. Sprinkle with seasoning salt.

2. Bake in preheated oven for 15 to 20 minutes, turning sweet potatoes halfway through, until crispy.

Variations

If you love fall flavors, substitute cinnamon sugar or pumpkin pie spice for the seasoning salt.

If you enjoy a little heat, add a pinch of ground cayenne pepper or curry powder with the seasoning salt.

Sweet Potato Noodle Bun

These handy-dandy little gems are a surprising way to eliminate a traditional bun. They are crunchy, tasty and gluten-free. You will find yourself making these buns and their variations for all of your sandwiches, burgers and breakfast sandwiches.

**MAKES
2 BUN HALVES**

Tip

Store cooked noodle buns, wrapped individually in plastic wrap, in the refrigerator for up to 2 days. Or prepare through step 3, then refrigerate for up to 24 hours before cooking.

Variation

Instead of the sweet potatoes, you can use russet potatoes, rutabagas or kohlrabi. Cook each of these for 5 to 7 minutes or until softened.

▶ **Two ¾-cup (175 mL) ramekins, sprayed with nonstick cooking spray**

1	sweet potato, peeled and ends cut flat	1
2 tsp	olive oil, divided	10 mL
1	large egg	1
Pinch	kosher salt	Pinch
Pinch	freshly ground black pepper	Pinch

1. Using a spiralizer, cut sweet potato into thin strands.
2. In a large skillet, heat ½ tsp (2 mL) oil over medium heat. Add sweet potato and cook, stirring, for 5 to 7 minutes or until softened. Let cool to room temperature, about 15 minutes.
3. In a medium bowl, whisk egg. Stir in sweet potato, salt and pepper. Divide between prepared ramekins, filling each about halfway and pressing the sweet potato down into the ramekins. Cover with plastic wrap and place a heavy can or jar on top of the wrap to weigh down the sweet potato. Refrigerate for 30 minutes.
4. Lightly coat a skillet with the remaining oil and heat over medium-high heat. Remove plastic wrap and invert ramekins to slide noodle buns onto skillet. Cook, turning once, for 3 to 5 minutes per side or until golden brown on both sides and hot in the center.

Variation

The seasoning combinations for these buns are endless. Add seasonings to the whisked egg before you add the sweet potato. Some of my favorites are: 2 tsp (10 mL) chopped fresh chives; a pinch each of ground allspice, cinnamon and ginger; 1 tsp (5 mL) each ground coriander and lime juice; 1 tsp (5 mL) each chopped pecans and pure maple syrup; seasoning salt or garlic powder to taste.

Potato Noodles au Gratin

This quick and easy recipe makes an excellent accompaniment to beef, pork or chicken. A great make-ahead dish, it can be reheated in the oven when you are ready to serve.

Tip

This recipe can be prepared and baked ahead of time. Let cool to room temperature, cover with plastic wrap, then foil, and refrigerate for up to 2 days. To serve, uncover and warm in a 325°F (160°C) oven for 30 to 40 minutes or until heated through.

▸ **Preheat oven to 425°F (220°C)**
▸ **10-cup (2.5 L) casserole dish, greased**

4	large russet potatoes, peeled and ends cut flat	4
Pinch	kosher salt	Pinch
Pinch	freshly ground black pepper	Pinch
½ cup	cream cheese	125 mL
¼ cup	butter	60 mL
½ cup	half-and-half (10%) cream	125 mL
2 cups	shredded sharp (old) Cheddar cheese, divided	500 mL
1½ tbsp	garlic powder	22 mL
2 tsp	onion powder	10 mL
½ cup	freshly grated Parmesan cheese (optional)	125 mL
2	green onions, sliced	2

1. Using a spiralizer, cut potatoes into wide ribbons. Place in prepared casserole dish and season with salt and pepper.

2. In a large skillet, melt cream cheese and butter over medium heat. Gradually add cream, stirring continuously. Add 1 cup (250 mL) Cheddar, garlic powder and onion powder, stirring until melted and well blended. Spoon over potatoes and cover with foil.

3. Bake in preheated oven for 35 minutes. Remove foil and top with the remaining Cheddar. Sprinkle with Parmesan (if using). Bake for 20 to 25 minutes or until potatoes are tender and cheese is bubbling. Serve sprinkled with green onions.

Bacon, Chive and Parmesan Potato Bake

Golden and bubbly, this dish is a perfect side dish for roasted pork. Any leftovers are perfect for your main course lunch.

Tip

Yellow-fleshed potatoes are often small, so they are a bit challenging to spiralize, but I do love their flavor and the nice curls they make. Peeled russet potatoes can be substituted, if desired.

▶ **Preheat oven to 350°F (180°C)**

▶ **9-inch (23 cm) square glass baking dish, sprayed with nonstick cooking spray**

2 tbsp	chopped fresh chives	30 mL
1 tsp	dried thyme	5 mL
1½ tsp	kosher salt	7 mL
¼ tsp	freshly ground black pepper	1 mL
½ cup	mayonnaise	125 mL
¼ cup	whole milk	60 mL
5 tbsp	freshly grated Parmesan cheese, divided	75 mL
12 oz	yellow-fleshed potatoes (unpeeled), ends cut flat	375 g
8 oz	sliced bacon, cooked crisp and crumbled	250 g

1. In a medium bowl, combine chives, thyme, salt, pepper, mayonnaise, milk and 3 tbsp (45 mL) cheese. Set aside.

2. Using a spiralizer, cut potatoes into wide ribbons. Place potatoes and bacon in prepared baking dish. Evenly spoon mayonnaise mixture over top. Sprinkle with the remaining cheese.

3. Bake in preheated oven for 20 to 25 minutes or until golden brown and bubbling.

Variation

Replace the bacon with 6 oz (175 g) cooked chopped pancetta.

Paleo Recipes

Beet, Radish and Apple Slaw

This colorful, zesty slaw delivers a refreshing surprise either as a side salad or in a fresh, crisp lettuce wrap.

Tips

If you cannot find Thai basil, you can substitute 1 tsp (5 mL) ground star anise. Star anise adds a hint of licorice flavor to this dish. Do not use sweet or regular basil, as their flavors are decidedly different.

When handling beets, you may want to wear kitchen gloves so you don't discolor your hands. Wash your spiralizer immediately after cutting beets to avoid discoloration.

Use one yellow beet and one red beet for added color and interest.

Try using 1 small daikon radish instead of red radishes.

5	large red radishes, ends cut flat	5
2	beets, peeled and ends cut flat	2
1	tart green apple (such as Granny Smith), cored	1
⅓ cup	chopped fresh cilantro	75 mL
2 tbsp	slivered fresh Thai basil leaves (see tip, at left)	30 mL
1½ tbsp	minced gingerroot	22 mL
¼ cup	rice vinegar (see tip, page 114)	60 mL
2 tsp	finely grated orange zest	10 mL
2 tsp	coconut amino acids	10 mL
	Kosher salt (optional)	
	Romaine lettuce leaves	

1. Using a spiralizer, cut radishes, beets and apple into thin strands. Transfer strands to a large bowl.

2. In a small bowl, combine cilantro, basil, ginger, vinegar, orange zest and coconut amino acids. Pour over strands and toss to coat. Season to taste with salt (if using). Let stand for 3 to 5 minutes to blend the flavors.

3. Line plates with lettuce and top with slaw. Wrap lettuce leaves around slaw, if desired.

Pacific Island Chicken and Broccoli Slaw

The secret to this simple slaw is the varied tastes and textures of lime, sesame seeds, ginger, cilantro and crunchy cashews, all giving a gracious nod to the islands of the Pacific.

MAKES 8 SERVINGS

Tips

Extra virgin olive oil is considered a healthy oil and is not inflammatory, so it is generally accepted in the paleo diet.

Tahini, a paste made from ground sesame seeds, is a popular ingredient in Middle Eastern and North African cuisine but works just as wonderfully in this Pacific Island–inspired dish.

Check the label on your tahini to make sure it was processed in a facility that either processes only sesame seeds or does not contain any gluten or nut cross-contamination (if you have allergies to specific nuts).

4	broccoli stems, peeled	4
2	carrots, peeled and ends cut flat	2
½	small red onion, peeled and ends cut flat	½
1	cucumber, ends cut flat	1
⅔ cup	extra virgin olive oil (see tip, at left), divided	150 mL
2 lbs	boneless skinless chicken breasts, cubed	1 kg
2 tbsp	toasted sesame seeds (see tip, page 88)	30 mL
1 tsp	grated gingerroot	5 mL
¼ cup	freshly squeezed lime juice	60 mL
3 tbsp	organic tahini	45 mL
2 tbsp	raw honey	30 mL
½ cup	chopped fresh cilantro	125 mL
¼ cup	cashew halves or pieces	60 mL

1. Using a spiralizer, cut broccoli stems, carrots and onion into medium strands. Cut cucumber into wide ribbons and pat dry. Trim strands and ribbons into 3-inch (7.5 cm) lengths. Set aside.

2. In a large skillet, heat 2 tbsp (30 mL) oil over medium heat. Add chicken and cook, stirring, for 5 to 7 minutes or until no longer pink inside. Transfer chicken to a plate and let cool.

3. In a jar with a tight-fitting lid, combine sesame seeds, ginger, the remaining oil, lime juice, tahini and honey. Cover tightly and shake until well blended.

4. In a large serving bowl, toss chicken, broccoli, carrots, onion, cucumber, cilantro and cashews. Pour dressing over salad mixture and toss to coat.

Mixed Vegetable Salad with Lemon Sesame Dressing

This simple, colorful and delicious salad pairs well with poultry or fish and is equally satisfying served by itself for a light lunch.

MAKES 4 SERVINGS

Tips

Sesame oil is considered a healthy oil and is not inflammatory, so it is generally accepted in the paleo diet.

Toast sesame seeds in a small skillet over medium-high heat for 3 to 4 minutes or until fragrant.

Parsnips, turnips or rutabaga, or a combination, can be substituted for the kohlrabi. You will need about 2 cups (500 mL) of spiralized vegetables.

4	carrots, peeled and ends cut flat	4
2	kohlrabi, peeled and ends cut flat	2
1	red onion, peeled and ends cut flat	1
2 tsp	finely minced garlic	10 mL
1 tsp	kosher salt	5 mL
1 tsp	freshly ground white pepper	5 mL
3 tbsp	freshly squeezed lemon juice	45 mL
1 tbsp	Dijon mustard	15 mL
½ cup	sesame oil	125 mL
1 tbsp	sesame seeds, toasted (see tip, at left)	15 mL

1. Using a spiralizer, cut carrots, kohlrabi and onion into medium strands. Transfer strands to a medium serving bowl.

2. In a small bowl, whisk together garlic, salt, pepper, lemon juice and mustard. Whisk in oil. Pour over the vegetables and toss to coat. Sprinkle with sesame seeds.

Green Bean and Butternut Pasta Salad with Lemon Thyme Dressing

A delightful crunch of pistachios gives green beans and butternut squash added dimension. Pair that with a zesty lemon thyme dressing and you have an all-star salad.

MAKES 4 SERVINGS

Tips

Phytic acid, found in legumes, can wreak havoc on our guts. However, green beans contain only trace amounts, if any, and are generally accepted on the paleo diet.

The bulbous end of the butternut squash can be used in a variety of ways. Try roasting it or using it to make soup.

▶ Steamer basket

1	butternut squash neck (at least 4 inches/10 cm long)	1
	Ice water	
8 oz	small green beans (see tip, at left), cut in half lengthwise	250 g
	Grated zest and juice of 1 lemon	
1	clove garlic, minced	1
1 tbsp	minced shallots	15 mL
1 tbsp	chopped fresh thyme	15 mL
½ tsp	kosher salt	2 mL
3 tbsp	sesame oil (see tip, page 88)	45 mL
¼ cup	chopped roasted pistachios	60 mL
2 cups	loosely packed arugula	500 mL

1. Peel squash neck and trim to 4 inches (10 cm) long, with flat ends. Using a spiralizer, cut squash into medium strands. Cut strands into 4-inch (10 cm) lengths.

2. In a steamer basket set over a saucepan of boiling water, steam squash for 5 to 7 minutes or until cooked to desired tenderness. Using a slotted spoon, immediately transfer squash to a bowl of ice water.

3. Add green beans to the steamer basket and steam for 3 to 5 minutes or until cooked to desired tenderness. Using a slotted spoon, immediately transfer beans to a bowl of ice water.

4. Drain squash and beans and pat dry. Transfer to a large serving bowl and toss with lemon zest.

5. In a small bowl, whisk together garlic, shallots, thyme, salt and lemon juice. Add oil in a slow, steady stream, whisking constantly. Stir in pistachios.

6. Add arugula to squash mixture. Drizzle with dressing and toss gently to coat.

Baked Salmon Salad with Curly Radishes

This is a perfect salad for a warm summer day or a garden party. The salad is colorful and crisp, and the salmon adds just the right touch.

MAKES 4 SERVINGS

Tips

Radishes come in an array of colors, shapes, sizes and flavors. While this recipe calls for red radishes, you can choose other varieties — just choose large radishes that are carrot-shaped for best results, otherwise they will not work in your spiralizer. Colorful radishes that complement the colors of the other ingredients will add extra pizazz to your salad.

When spiralizing, you always end up with a little bit of vegetable or fruit that is too small to spiralize. I use these pieces to taste-test my dressing before adding it to the salad.

▶ **Preheat oven to 350°F (180°C)**
▶ **13- by 9-inch (33 by 23 cm) glass baking dish, greased**

1 lb	salmon fillet	500 g
1 tbsp	extra virgin olive oil (see tip, page 87)	15 mL
Pinch	kosher salt	Pinch
	Freshly ground black pepper	
3	large red radishes, ends cut flat	3
2	cucumbers (peeled or unpeeled), ends cut flat	2
1	carrot, peeled and ends cut flat	1
1	large shallot, minced	1
¼ cup	minced fresh dill	60 mL
2 tbsp	cider vinegar (see tip, page 114)	30 mL
1½ tbsp	sesame oil (see tip, page 88)	22 mL
1 tbsp	water	15 mL
2 tsp	balsamic vinegar	10 mL
6 cups	packed mesclun mix or mixed baby greens	1.5 L
1 cup	cherry tomatoes, halved	250 mL

1. Place salmon, skin side down, in prepared baking dish. Brush top of salmon with oil. Season salmon with salt and a pinch of pepper. Bake in preheated oven for 25 to 30 minutes or until salmon is opaque and flakes easily when tested with a fork. Let cool. Discard skin and flake salmon into medium pieces.

Tip

Cucumbers have a high water content. Pat the ribbons dry as much as possible before adding them to your salad. You can also sprinkle them lightly with salt, place them in a colander and let them drain for 15 minutes (or while you are preparing the other ingredients).

2. Meanwhile, using a spiralizer, cut radishes and cucumbers into wide ribbons and pat cucumber ribbons dry. Cut carrot into thin strands. Trim all ribbons and strands into 4-inch (10 cm) lengths.

3. In a medium bowl, whisk together shallot, dill, cider vinegar, oil, water and balsamic vinegar.

4. Divide mesclun mix among four plates. Scatter one-quarter each of the salmon, radishes, cucumbers, carrots and tomatoes on each plate. Drizzle dressing over salad and serve. If desired, sprinkle with pepper.

Cabbage and Veggie Soup

If you are craving comfort food, this hearty central and eastern European soup will warm you up on a cold day. Our version is *kapustnik*, made with raw cabbage. We have also included a variation for *kapusniak*, made with sauerkraut.

Tip

Potatoes are often excluded from paleo-approved food lists because of their high carbohydrate and starch content. If you experience blood sugar spikes or have an autoimmune disorder, you may want to skip this recipe.

Variations

Kapusniak: Replace the cabbage with 1 lb (500 g) sauerkraut, drained. For a tangier soup, reserve the juice and add it to the soup in step 3.

Sausage, Cabbage and Veggie Soup: Add 1 lb (500 g) Polish sausage, such as kielbasa, cut diagonally into 1-inch (2.5 cm) slices. Add with the tomatoes in step 3.

4	carrots, peeled and ends cut flat	4
2	russet potatoes (see tip, at left), peeled and ends cut flat	2
1	onion, peeled and ends cut flat	1
1	head cabbage, outer leaves removed, cut in half and ends cut flat	1
4	slices thick-cut bacon, coarsely chopped	4
2	stalks celery, thinly sliced	2
2	cloves garlic, minced	2
3 tbsp	minced reconstituted sun-dried tomatoes	45 mL
2 tsp	Hungarian paprika	10 mL
1	bay leaf	1
8 cups	ready-to-use reduced-sodium beef broth	2 L
	Chopped fresh parsley (optional)	
	Sour cream (optional)	

1. Using a spiralizer, cut carrots, potatoes and onion into medium strands. Cut cabbage into wide ribbons, keeping them separate. Set aside.

2. In a Dutch oven, cook bacon over medium heat, stirring, until softened but not crisp. Add carrots, potatoes, onion, celery and garlic; cook, stirring, for 5 to 7 minutes or until onion is translucent. Add cabbage and cook, stirring, for 5 to 7 minutes or until just wilted.

3. Stir in tomatoes, paprika, bay leaf and broth; increase heat to medium-high and bring to a boil, stirring. Reduce heat and simmer, stirring occasionally, for 10 minutes or until vegetables are cooked to desired tenderness. Discard bay leaf. Serve immediately, garnished with parsley and sour cream, if desired.

Zesty Shrimp and Squash Vermicelli Soup

This one-pot dish pairs a little heat from chile peppers with the slightly sweet taste of butternut squash. Top that with shrimp and you have a flavorful, comforting dish.

MAKES 4 SERVINGS

Tips

Choose chiles that are soft and not dried out. Ancho chiles should have a slightly sweet, smoky smell similar to raisins or figs.

Wear kitchen gloves when working with chiles. Avoid touching your face or anything other than what you need to chop the chiles.

Conventional thinking is that dairy products are forbidden on the paleo diet; however, many followers feel that a moderate amount of dairy is not detrimental, particularly in the case of fermented milk products, such as sour cream and yogurt, which contain friendly bacteria that can improve digestion and gut health. The sour cream or yogurt is optional in this soup, but does improve the results.

2	dried ancho chile peppers, stems and seeds removed	2
	Hot water	
2	butternut squash necks (at least 4 inches/10 cm long)	2
2 tbsp	extra virgin olive oil (see tip, page 87)	30 mL
1	onion, chopped	1
2	cloves garlic, minced	2
1 tsp	ground sage	5 mL
1 tsp	ground cumin	5 mL
4 cups	ready-to-use reduced-sodium chicken broth	1 L
1 lb	medium shrimp (31 to 35 count), peeled and deveined	500 g
1/4 cup	chopped fresh cilantro	60 mL
1/2 cup	sour cream or yogurt (optional; see tip, at left)	125 mL

1. Soak chiles in hot water for 5 to 10 minutes or until softened. Drain and chop.

2. Meanwhile, peel butternut squash necks and trim to 4 inches (10 cm) long, with flat ends. Using a spiralizer, cut squash into thin strands. Set aside.

3. In a Dutch oven, heat oil over medium heat. Add onion and cook, stirring, for 3 to 4 minutes or until softened. Add garlic, sage and cumin; cook, stirring, for 1 minute or until onions are light golden and garlic is fragrant.

4. Stir in chiles and broth; bring to a simmer. Add squash, reduce heat and simmer for 5 to 7 minutes or until just starting to soften. Add shrimp and cook, stirring, for 2 to 3 minutes or until shrimp are pink, firm and opaque and squash is cooked to desired tenderness. Serve immediately, garnished with cilantro and sour cream (if using).

Paleo Zuppa Toscana

Get ready to please the whole family. This creamy, flavorful Italian soup is the crowning glory of dinner-time favorites.

**MAKES
4 SERVINGS**

Tips

Check to be sure that the sausage you buy is certified gluten-free or has been packaged in a facility where there is no gluten cross-contamination.

You can use gluten-free sausage in casings and remove the casings before cooking. Check the packaging to make sure there are no added ingredients that are not paleo-friendly.

If you like heat, you can add more hot pepper flakes to taste. This soup will get spicier as it simmers, so add small amounts at first.

4	turnips, peeled and ends cut flat	4
1	onion, peeled and ends cut flat	1
1 lb	Italian sausage (bulk or casings removed)	500 g
3	cloves garlic, minced	3
Pinch	hot pepper flakes	Pinch
8 cups	ready-to-use reduced-sodium chicken broth	2 L
4 cups	chopped kale leaves	1 L
1 cup	unsweetened almond milk	250 mL
	Kosher salt	
	Freshly ground black pepper	

1. Using a spiralizer, cut turnips into thin strands. Cut onion into medium strands, keeping them separate. Set aside.

2. In a large saucepan, cook sausage over medium-high heat, breaking it up with a spoon, for 7 to 9 minutes or until no longer pink. Add onion strands, garlic and hot pepper flakes to taste; cook, stirring, for 3 to 5 minutes or until onion is softened.

3. Add broth and bring to a boil, stirring. Reduce heat to low, add kale and cook, stirring, for 2 minutes. Add turnips and milk; cook, stirring gently, for 2 to 3 minutes or until turnips and kale are cooked to desired tenderness. Season to taste with salt and black pepper.

Salmon with Creamy Dill Sauce over Celery Root Noodles

You will delight in this new flavor dimension of celery root noodles and salmon paired with a refreshing, creamy dill sauce. No one need know how quick and easy this dish is to prepare.

**MAKES
4 SERVINGS**

Tips

Celery root is difficult to spiralize because of its harder consistency. Don't be concerned if your ribbons become half-moon-shaped or break into shorter strips; they will still be delicious.

Instead of baking the celery root ribbons, steam them for a different texture and an incredible aroma. Steam for 3 to 5 minutes just before the salmon is done roasting.

Add 2 tbsp (30 mL) drained capers to the sauce in step 1 for an additional taste sensation.

▸ **Preheat oven to 375°F (190°C), with one rack in the upper third and one in the bottom third**
▸ **Baking sheet, lined with parchment paper**
▸ **13- by 9-inch (33 by 23 cm) glass baking dish, greased**

¾ cup	plain Greek yogurt (see tip, page 93)	175 mL
1 tbsp	chopped fresh dill	15 mL
1 tsp	grated lemon zest	5 mL
1 tbsp	freshly squeezed lemon juice	15 mL
3	celery roots, peeled and ends cut flat	3
3 tbsp	extra virgin olive oil (see tip, page 97), divided	45 mL
1 lb	salmon fillet, cut into 4 equal pieces	500 g
	Kosher salt	
	Freshly ground black pepper	

1. In a small bowl, combine yogurt, dill, lemon zest and lemon juice. Set aside.

2. Using a spiralizer, cut celery roots into wide ribbons. Arrange ribbons on prepared baking sheet and drizzle with 1 tbsp (15 mL) oil. Set aside.

3. Brush salmon on both sides with the remaining oil. Lay salmon, skin side down, in prepared baking dish. Season with salt and pepper. Bake on upper rack of preheated oven for 5 minutes. Add the baking sheet of celery root ribbons to the lower rack of the oven and bake for 15 to 17 minutes or until salmon is opaque and flakes easily when tested with a fork and celery root is cooked to desired tenderness.

4. Divide celery root among four plates and drizzle with dill sauce, using half the sauce. Place salmon on celery root. Serve immediately, with the remaining dill sauce on the side.

Tilapia and Zucchini Pasta with Mustard Cream Sauce

You will swoon over this dreamy mustard cream sauce served over delicate tilapia and zucchini noodles. Cool lime kicks the flavors up a notch.

**MAKES
2 SERVINGS**

Tips

Choose zucchini that are straight and fairly even in diameter. This will make it easier to spiral-cut them evenly.

▶ **Preheat oven to 400°F (200°C)**
▶ **Baking sheet, lined with parchment paper**

3	zucchini, ends cut flat	3
2	skinless tilapia fillets (about 10 oz/300 g total)	2
1	lime, cut in half	1
	Kosher salt	
	Freshly ground black pepper	
½ cup	ready-to-use chicken broth	125 mL
2 tbsp	Dijon mustard	30 mL
2 tsp	ground coriander	10 mL
1 tsp	ground cumin	5 mL
2 tbsp	coconut milk	30 mL

1. Using a spiralizer, cut zucchini into wide ribbons. Set aside.

2. Place tilapia on prepared baking sheet. Squeeze lime juice over each fillet. Season with salt and pepper. Bake in preheated oven for 10 to 15 minutes or until tilapia is opaque and flakes easily when tested with a fork.

3. Meanwhile, in a large skillet, combine broth, mustard, coriander and cumin. Bring to a simmer. Stir in coconut milk. Add zucchini and cook, stirring, for 2 to 3 minutes or until cooked to desired tenderness.

4. Using tongs, transfer zucchini to serving plates. Lay tilapia over zucchini. Pour cream sauce over top.

Variation

If you like a bit of crunchy coating on your fish, combine 1 tbsp (15 mL) each coconut flour and dried parsley with the salt and pepper before seasoning. Sprinkle onto fish and pat down.

VEGETABLES PREPPED FOR THE SPIRALIZER

Sweet Potato

Cucumber

Parsnips

Carrots

Beet

Broccoli Stems

Zucchini

Butternut Squash

SPIRALIZED VEGETABLES AND FRUITS

FINE STRANDS

Beets

Potato

Butternut Squash

Kohlrabi

Carrot

Turnip

THIN STRANDS

Zucchini

Beets

Plantain

Butternut Squash

Jicama

Sweet Potato

SPIRALIZED VEGETABLES AND FRUITS

MEDIUM STRANDS

WIDE RIBBONS

Apple

Celery Root

Sweet Potato

Carrot

Daikon Radish

Butternut Squash

Beets

Kohlrabi

Cucumber

Carrot

Red Pepper

Pear

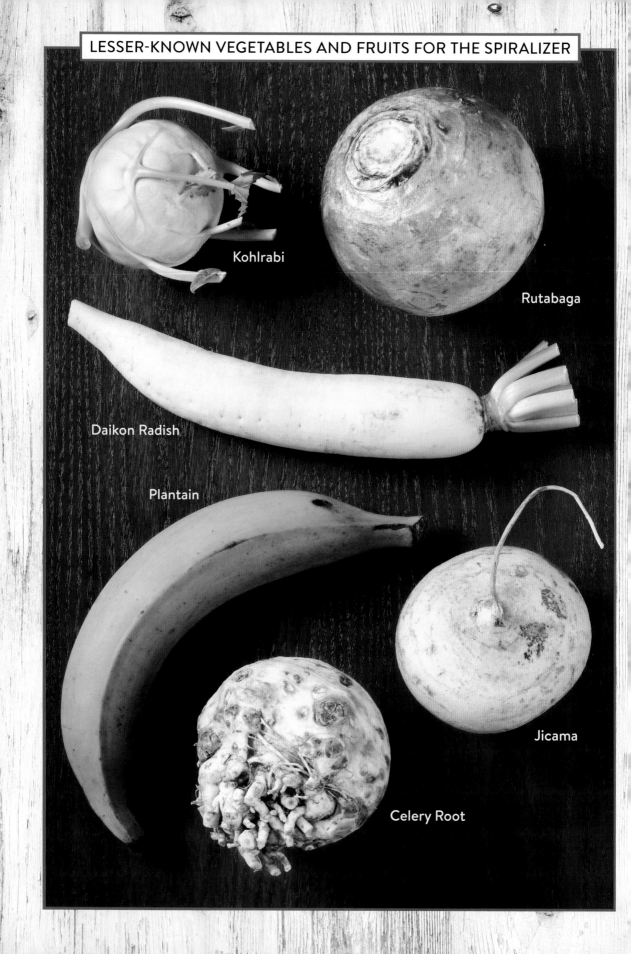

Kohlrabi

Rutabaga

Daikon Radish

Plantain

Jicama

Celery Root

Chicken and Tangy Peanut Sauce over Squash and Carrot Noodles (page 53)

Creamy Alfredo Vegetable Pasta with Prosciutto and Peas (page 72)

Sweet Potato Noodle Bun (page 82)

Zesty Shrimp and Squash Vermicelli Soup (page 93)

Savory Crab, Asparagus and Veggie Noodles

This delicate crab and asparagus dish could easily become your go-to dish for a quick, easy and decadent weeknight dinner or a special evening meal with friends.

MAKES 4 SERVINGS

Tips

Extra virgin olive oil is considered a healthy oil and is not inflammatory, so it is generally accepted in the paleo diet.

To make ⅓ cup (75 mL) Paleo Parmesan, a replacement for Parmesan cheese, in a food processor, process ⅓ cup (75 mL) whole raw almonds, 1 tbsp (15 mL) nutritional yeast and a pinch of kosher salt until fluffy and no chunks of nuts remain.

4	zucchini, ends cut flat	4
3 tbsp	extra virgin olive oil (see tip, at left)	45 mL
3	cloves garlic, minced	3
Pinch	hot pepper flakes	Pinch
1 cup	ready-to-use vegetable broth	250 mL
	Grated zest and juice of 1 small lemon	
1 lb	asparagus, trimmed and cut diagonally into 2-inch (5 cm) pieces	500 g
1 lb	frozen cooked crabmeat, thawed	500 g
¼ cup	chopped fresh parsley (optional)	60 mL
	Kosher salt and freshly ground black pepper (optional)	
⅓ cup	Paleo Parmesan (see tip, at left)	75 mL

1. Using a spiralizer, cut zucchini into thin strands. Set aside.

2. In a large skillet, heat oil over medium heat. Add garlic, hot pepper flakes, broth and lemon juice; cook, stirring occasionally, for about 10 minutes or until liquid is reduced by half. Add asparagus and cook, stirring, for about 5 minutes or until just tender-crisp.

3. Gently stir in crab, lemon zest and zucchini; cook, stirring, for 2 to 3 minutes or until cooked to desired tenderness. If desired, toss with parsley, salt and pepper. Serve immediately, sprinkled with Paleo Parmesan.

Grilled Scallop Tacos and Cabbage Slaw with Spicy Avocado Sauce

You will enjoy the surprise flavors in this dish of delicate seared scallops topped with a crunchy veggie slaw and spicy avocado, all nicely wrapped in a cauliflower tortilla.

MAKES 6 SERVINGS

Tips

Most varieties of cabbage with tightly packed leaves work well in the spiralizer. I have had the best results with red and green cabbage.

Extra virgin olive oil is considered a healthy oil and is not inflammatory, so it is generally accepted in the paleo diet.

▸ **Preheat oven to 375°F (190°C)**
▸ **Food processor**
▸ **Colander, lined with cheesecloth, or nut milk bag**
▸ **Baking sheet, lined with parchment paper**

Cauliflower Tortillas

1	small head cauliflower, florets only	1
2	large eggs, beaten	2
1 tsp	dried oregano	5 mL
Pinch	kosher salt	Pinch
Pinch	freshly ground black pepper	Pinch

Spicy Avocado Sauce

1	large avocado, chopped	1
1	jalapeño pepper, minced (see tip, opposite)	1
1	clove garlic, minced	1
1/4 cup	coarsely chopped fresh cilantro	60 mL
	Kosher salt	
	Freshly ground black pepper	
1/2 cup	water	125 mL
1 tbsp	freshly squeezed lime juice	15 mL

Taco Filling

1	small cabbage, outer leaves removed, ends cut flat	1
1	small red onion, peeled and ends cut flat	1
1	small jicama, peeled and ends cut flat	1
1 1/2 tsp	coarsely chopped fresh cilantro	7 mL
1 to 2 tbsp	extra virgin olive oil (see tip, at left)	15 to 30 mL
12 oz	small sea scallops (50 to 60 count)	375 g
2	cloves garlic, minced	2

Tips

For a milder avocado sauce, remove some or all of the seeds from the jalapeño.

After removing the scallops from the skillet, you can individually add each tortilla to the skillet for about 15 seconds to reheat them before assembling the tacos.

1. *Tortillas:* In food processor, pulse cauliflower until it resembles damp grains. You should have about 2 cups (500 mL).

2. Transfer cauliflower to a microwave-safe bowl, cover, leaving a small opening to allow steam to escape, and microwave on High for 4 minutes. Carefully pour cauliflower into prepared colander and let drain and cool. Twist the cheesecloth to squeeze out as much liquid as possible.

3. Return cauliflower to the bowl and add eggs, oregano, salt and pepper. Using your hands, work mixture into a dough-like consistency.

4. Divide dough into 6 equal balls and place on prepared baking sheet. Flatten balls into circles about $1/4$ inch (0.5 cm) thick.

5. Bake in preheated oven for 8 to 10 minutes or until lightly browned. Flip tortillas and bake for 5 minutes or until browned and firm.

6. *Sauce:* In food processor, combine avocado, jalapeño, garlic, cilantro, salt and pepper to taste, water and lime juice; process until smooth. Transfer to a small serving bowl, cover and set aside.

7. *Filling:* Using a spiralizer, cut cabbage and onion into medium strands. Cut jicama into thin strands and pat dry. In a bowl, toss together cabbage, onion, jicama and cilantro.

8. In a large skillet, heat 1 tbsp (30 mL) oil over medium-high heat. Working in batches, add scallops and cook, turning once, for 1 minute per side or until firm and opaque, adding more oil and adjusting heat as necessary between batches. Immediately arrange scallops on tortillas, dividing evenly. Top with cabbage mixture and avocado sauce.

Variation

Grilled Chicken Tacos: Substitute 12 oz (375 g) chicken breasts, cubed, for the scallops. In step 8, cook chicken, stirring, until no longer pink inside.

Spanish-Inspired Shrimp and Scallops with Butternut Squash

This dish has all the flavors you would expect in a traditional paella, but with butternut squash noodles instead of rice for a unique twist.

**MAKES
6 SERVINGS**

Tips

The bulbous end of the butternut squash contains seeds, so it does not spiralize well. Try roasting it instead, for a luscious side dish with any meal. Peel the squash, remove seeds and cut into 1½-inch (4 cm) cubes. Toss with melted butter, brown sugar, salt and pepper and roast in a 400°F (200°C) oven for 20 to 25 minutes.

Extra virgin olive oil is considered a healthy oil and is not inflammatory, so it is generally accepted in the paleo diet.

▶ **14- to 16-inch (36 to 40 cm) paella pan or shallow skillet**

2	butternut squash necks (at least 4 inches/10 cm long)	2
1	onion, peeled and ends cut flat	1
3 tbsp	extra virgin olive oil (see tip, at left), divided	45 mL
12 oz	extra-large shrimp (16 to 20 count), peeled and deveined	375 g
12 oz	sea scallops (20 to 30 count)	375 g
1	cured chorizo sausage (about 3 oz/90 g), thickly sliced	1
2	cloves garlic, minced	2
2 cups	diced peeled tomatoes (about 1½ lbs/750 g)	500 mL
1 tsp	kosher salt	5 mL
¼ tsp	smoked paprika	1 mL
¼ tsp	freshly ground black pepper	1 mL
2 to 3	saffron threads	2 to 3
1¾ cups	ready-to-use reduced-sodium chicken broth	425 mL
¼ cup	chopped fresh parsley (optional)	60 mL

1. Peel butternut squash necks and trim to 4 inches (10 cm) long, with flat ends. Using a spiralizer, cut squash into thin strands. Trim strands into finger lengths. Cut onion into medium strands, keeping them separate. Set aside.

Tips

Traditional paella has a toasted rice bottom called socarrat. This bottom forms with the traditional Arborio rice and also with the squash noodles. Don't be concerned if your noodles are sticking to the bottom of the pan, as long as they are getting toasted and not burned.

If you like the rice presentation of paella, pulse the spiralized squash noodles in a food processor a few times to create "rice."

2. In paella pan, heat 2 tbsp (30 mL) oil over medium-high heat. Add shrimp and cook, stirring, for 2 to 3 minutes or until pink, firm and opaque. Using a slotted spoon, transfer shrimp to a plate.

3. Working in batches, add scallops and cook, turning once, for 1 minute per side or until firm and opaque, adjusting heat as necessary between batches. Transfer scallops to plate with shrimp.

4. Add chorizo to the pan and cook, stirring, for 2 to 3 minutes or until starting to brown. Reduce heat to medium and add the remaining oil. Add onion strands, garlic, tomatoes, salt, paprika, pepper and saffron; cook, stirring, for 5 to 7 minutes or until onions are translucent.

5. Add broth, scraping up any browned bits from the bottom of the pan. Stir in squash strands, reduce heat and simmer, stirring, for 4 to 6 minutes or until just tender. Return shrimp and scallops to the pan and simmer until heated through.

6. Serve in paella pan or transfer to a serving plate. If desired, garnish with parsley.

Grilled Shrimp with Zucchini Noodles and Lemon Basil Dressing

Ready in just minutes, this light and easy main dish is a perfect weeknight meal.

Tips

To toast sliced almonds, spread them in a small skillet and cook over medium-high heat, stirring for 2 to 3 minutes or until just browned.

Perfectly cooked shrimp are firm, slightly pink and form the letter C. It is very easy to overcook shrimp, so watch them carefully. Unlike some foods that become more tender with additional cooking, overcooked shrimp are tough.

▶ **Blender or food processor**

5	zucchini, ends cut flat		5
2	cloves garlic, coarsely chopped		2
1	shallot, coarsely chopped		1
2 cups	fresh basil		500 mL
1/3 cup	toasted sliced almonds, divided (see tip, at left)		75 mL
1/4 tsp	hot pepper flakes		1 mL
	Grated zest of 1 lemon		
5 tbsp	extra virgin olive oil (see tip, page 103), divided		75 mL
1 tbsp	red wine vinegar (see tip, page 114)		15 mL
1 lb	large shrimp (26 to 30 count), peeled and deveined		500 g
	Kosher salt		
	Freshly cracked black pepper		

1. Using a spiralizer, cut zucchini into thin strands. Set aside.

2. In blender, combine garlic, shallot, basil, 1/4 cup (60 mL) almonds, hot pepper flakes, lemon zest, 4 tbsp (60 mL) oil and vinegar; blend until smooth. Set aside.

3. In a medium skillet, heat the remaining oil over medium heat. Add shrimp and cook, stirring, for 2 to 3 minutes or until pink, firm and opaque. Remove from heat and stir in 2 tbsp (30 mL) of the lemon basil dressing. Using a slotted spoon, transfer shrimp to a plate and keep warm.

4. Add zucchini to the skillet and cook over medium heat, stirring, for 2 to 3 minutes or until cooked to desired tenderness. Add the remaining lemon basil dressing and toss to coat.

5. Divide zucchini evenly among four plates. Top with shrimp and season to taste with salt and pepper. Sprinkle with the remaining almonds.

Spicy Shrimp and Parsnip Noodles

This dish is a combination of spicy shrimp and seasonings on a bed of sweet parsnips, for a surprising and delectable taste combination you are sure to enjoy.

Tips

Extra virgin olive oil is considered a healthy oil and is not inflammatory, so it is generally accepted in the paleo diet.

To determine whether your shrimp are properly done, use the spring test: hold the head end of the shrimp and gently pull the tail down. If cooked properly, the tail will spring back.

5	parsnips, peeled and ends cut flat	5
3 tbsp	extra virgin olive oil (see tip, at left), divided	45 mL
1 cup	finely chopped onion	250 mL
3	cloves garlic, minced	3
¼ tsp	hot pepper flakes	1 mL
½ tsp	chili powder	2 mL
½ tsp	smoked paprika	2 mL
Pinch	kosher salt (optional)	Pinch
Pinch	freshly ground black pepper (optional)	Pinch
1 lb	large shrimp (26 to 30 count), peeled and deveined	500 g
½ cup	ready-to-use chicken broth	125 mL
2 tbsp	chopped fresh parsley (optional)	30 mL

1. Using a spiralizer, cut parsnips into wide ribbons. Set aside.

2. In a large skillet, heat 2 tbsp (30 mL) oil over medium heat. Add onion and cook, stirring, for 3 to 5 minutes or until translucent. Add garlic and hot pepper flakes; cook, stirring, for 30 seconds or until fragrant.

3. Add the remaining oil. Add parsnips, chili powder, paprika, salt (if using) and pepper (if using); cook, stirring, for 3 to 4 minutes or until parsnips are cooked to desired tenderness. Using tongs, transfer parsnips to a plate.

4. Add shrimp and broth to the skillet and cook, stirring, for 2 to 3 minutes or until shrimp are pink, firm and opaque. Return parsnips to the skillet and toss to combine. Serve immediately, garnished with parsley (if using).

Shrimp with Slow-Roasted Tomatoes and Zucchini Linguine

Slow-roasted tomatoes deliver a sweet, deep and exquisite flavor to the zucchini noodles and shrimp. Once you master slow-roasting tomatoes, you will never stop making these tasty little jewels.

Tips

Extra virgin olive oil is considered a healthy oil and is not inflammatory, so it is generally accepted in the paleo diet.

Perfectly cooked shrimp are firm, slightly pink and form the letter C. It is very easy to overcook shrimp, so watch them carefully. Unlike some foods that become more tender with additional cooking, overcooked shrimp are tough.

A spring test works well to determine if your shrimp are properly done: hold the head end and pull the tail down. If the shrimp is cooked correctly, the tail will spring back.

▸ **Preheat oven to 325°F (160°C)**
▸ **Rimmed baking sheet, lined with foil**

Slow-Roasted Tomatoes

2	cloves garlic, thinly sliced	2
1 tsp	dried thyme	5 mL
1 tsp	dried rosemary	5 mL
Pinch	kosher salt	Pinch
Pinch	freshly ground black pepper	Pinch
¼ cup	extra virgin olive oil (see tip, at left)	60 mL
2 lbs	plum (Roma) or cherry tomatoes, halved	1 kg

Shrimp and Linguine

5	zucchini, ends cut flat	5
2 tbsp	extra virgin olive oil	30 mL
4	cloves garlic, thinly sliced	4
Pinch	hot pepper flakes	Pinch
¾ cup	dry white wine	175 mL
Pinch	kosher salt	Pinch
1¼ lbs	extra-large shrimp (16 to 20 count), peeled and deveined	625 g
1½ cups	ready-to-use reduced-sodium chicken broth	375 mL

1. *Tomatoes:* In a large bowl, combine garlic, thyme, rosemary, salt, pepper and oil. Add tomatoes and toss to coat. Place tomatoes, cut side down, on prepared baking sheet. Bake in preheated oven for 2 hours or until softened and beginning to wrinkle.

Tip

Choose zucchini that are straight and fairly even in diameter. This will make it easier to spiral-cut them evenly.

2. *Shrimp and Linguine:* Using a spiralizer, cut zucchini into medium strands. Set aside.

3. In a large skillet, heat oil over medium-low heat. Add garlic and cook, stirring, for 30 seconds or until fragrant. Stir in roasted tomatoes and hot pepper flakes. Increase heat to medium-high, add wine and salt; cook, stirring, until bubbling. Add shrimp and cook, stirring, for 2 to 3 minutes or until pink, firm and opaque. Using a slotted spoon, transfer shrimp to a plate.

4. Reduce heat to medium, stir in broth and bring to a simmer. Add zucchini, reduce heat and simmer, stirring, for 1 to 3 minutes or until cooked to desired tenderness. Return shrimp to the skillet and toss to combine. Serve immediately.

Garlic and Herb Lemon Chicken with Roasted Spiral Squash

This flavorful chicken dish is the perfect quick-and-easy weeknight meal.

Tips

Choose delicata squash that are shorter in length. When you cut off the ends, use a long spoon to scoop out the seeds. Shorter squash will make this easier to do.

If your delicata squash have a thicker skin than you prefer, you can peel the skin before using. You can easily check the thickness of the skin once you have cut off the ends.

You can use butternut squash in place of the delicata. Use the neck of 1 medium butternut squash, peeled and trimmed to 4 inches (10 cm) long before spiralizing. Bake for 5 to 7 minutes or until cooked to desired tenderness.

▷ **Preheat oven to 400°F (200°C), with one rack in the upper third and one in the bottom third**

▷ **13- by 9-inch (33 by 23 cm) glass baking dish, lightly sprayed with nonstick cooking spray**

▷ **Baking sheet, lined with foil**

3 tbsp	extra virgin olive oil (see tip, page 104), divided	45 mL
4	boneless skinless chicken breasts (about 1 lb/500 g)	4
1½ tsp	dried parsley	7 mL
1 tsp	dried basil	5 mL
1 tsp	seasoned salt	5 mL
½ tsp	garlic powder	2 mL
½ tsp	freshly ground black pepper	2 mL
2	delicata squash, ends cut flat and seeds removed (see tips, at left)	2
Pinch	kosher salt	Pinch
1 tbsp	freshly squeezed lemon juice	15 mL
1 tbsp	chopped fresh parsley	15 mL

1. Using 1½ tbsp (22 mL) oil, brush both sides of chicken. Sprinkle both sides of chicken with dried parsley, basil, seasoned salt, garlic powder and pepper. Place in prepared baking dish. Bake on upper rack of preheated oven for 15 minutes.

2. Meanwhile, using a spiralizer, cut squash into medium strands. Place strands on prepared baking sheet and drizzle with the remaining oil. Sprinkle with kosher salt and toss to coat. Add to the lower rack of the oven and bake for 8 to 10 minutes, stirring squash halfway through, until chicken is no longer pink inside and squash is cooked to desired tenderness.

3. Transfer squash to a serving plate and top with chicken. Drizzle with lemon juice and sprinkle with fresh parsley.

French Country Noodles
with Lemon-Garlic Chicken

Zucchini noodles get an uplift in this twist on a classic French country dish with delectable lemon-and-garlic-marinated chicken.

	MAKES 2 SERVINGS	

Tips

Zest the remaining lemon half and let the zest air-dry overnight or until all moisture has evaporated. Store in an airtight container in a cool, dry place for 1 to 2 days. When using dried zest, measure half the amount of fresh zest called for in your recipe.

Ghee is a type of clarified butter with a nutty flavor. It contains virtually no lactose or milk proteins, so it doesn't cause the inflammation, sensitivities and intolerances that dairy products can. It is considered a healthy oil and has a high smoke point, so it is generally accepted in the paleo diet.

2	cloves garlic, minced	2
1 tbsp	minced fresh parsley	15 mL
	Kosher salt	
	Freshly ground black pepper	
1½ tsp	extra virgin olive oil (see tip, page 104)	7 mL
	Grated zest and juice of ½ lemon	
8 oz	boneless skinless chicken breasts, cut into strips	250 g
2	zucchini, ends cut flat	2
2 tbsp	ghee (see tip, at left)	30 mL
½ cup	ready-to-use reduced-sodium chicken broth	125 mL
	Additional chopped fresh parsley (optional)	

1. In a medium bowl, combine garlic, minced parsley, ½ tsp (2 mL) salt, ¼ tsp (1 mL) pepper, oil, lemon zest and lemon juice. Add chicken, cover and refrigerate for 30 minutes.

2. Meanwhile, using a spiralizer, cut zucchini into thin strands. Set aside.

3. In a medium skillet, melt ghee over medium-high heat. Transfer chicken to skillet, discarding any excess marinade, and cook, stirring, for 2 to 4 minutes or until chicken is no longer pink inside. Transfer chicken to a plate and keep warm.

4. Add broth to skillet, scraping up any browned bits from the bottom of the pan, and bring to a boil over medium-high heat. Add zucchini, reduce heat and simmer, stirring, for 2 to 3 minutes or until cooked to desired tenderness.

5. Divide zucchini between two plates and, if desired, season with a pinch of salt and pepper. Top with chicken. Sprinkle with chopped parsley, if desired. Serve immediately.

Chicken Scaloppini with Lemon Glaze and Zucchini Fettuccine

In this easy but elegant dish, chicken breasts get a gourmet touch with a lemon glaze and capers — a great topping for zucchini noodles.

Tips

If you don't have poultry seasoning on hand, you can use any preferred combination of ground sage, thyme and/ or marjoram.

Extra virgin olive oil is considered a healthy oil and is not inflammatory, so it is generally accepted in the paleo diet.

▶ **Meat mallet or rolling pin**

1 cup	almond flour	250 mL
½ tsp	garlic powder	2 mL
½ tsp	seasoned salt	2 mL
¼ tsp	poultry seasoning	1 mL
2	medium or large eggs	2
2 tbsp	Dijon mustard	30 mL
4	boneless skinless chicken breasts (about 1 lb/500 g)	4
2 tbsp	extra virgin olive oil (see tip, at left)	30 mL
4	zucchini, ends cut flat	4
¼ cup	ready-to-use chicken broth	60 mL
2½ tbsp	freshly squeezed lemon juice	37 mL
Pinch	kosher salt	Pinch
1 tbsp	chopped fresh parsley	15 mL
2 tsp	drained capers	10 mL

1. In a shallow dish, combine almond flour, garlic powder, seasoned salt and poultry seasoning. In a small bowl, whisk together eggs and mustard.

2. Place chicken on a cutting board, cover top and bottom with plastic wrap and, using the meat mallet, pound to about ¼ inch (0.5 cm) thick. Dredge chicken in egg mixture, shaking off any excess, then in flour mixture. Press flour mixture onto chicken to ensure it is well coated. Discard any excess egg mixture and flour mixture.

Tips

Choose zucchini that are straight and fairly even in diameter. This will make it easier to spiral-cut them evenly.

3. In a medium skillet, heat 1 tbsp (15 mL) oil over medium heat. Working in batches, add chicken and cook, turning once, for 3 to 5 minutes per side or until no longer pink inside, adding more oil and adjusting heat as necessary between batches. Transfer chicken to a plate and keep warm.

4. Using a spiralizer, cut zucchini into medium strands.

5. Return skillet to medium heat. Add broth, lemon juice and salt to the skillet, scraping up any browned bits from the bottom of the pan. Add zucchini, reduce heat and simmer for 1 to 2 minutes or until sauce is slightly thickened and zucchini is cooked to desired tenderness. Using tongs, transfer zucchini to a serving plate. Stir parsley and capers into glaze.

6. Place chicken on top of zucchini and spoon glaze over chicken. Serve immediately.

Mediterranean Chicken with Artichoke Hearts, Olives and Beets

Transport your dinner guests to the sun-kissed shores of the Mediterranean with artichoke hearts, olives and pine nuts floating over a delicate pairing of chicken and luscious yellow beets.

MAKES 4 SERVINGS

Tips

If you can't find yellow beets, you can use red beets in this recipe. However, to avoid turning the chicken and artichokes purple, you'll want to cook them in a separate pan. In step 3, bring an additional ½ cup (125 mL) ready-to-use chicken broth to a boil over medium-high heat. Add beets, reduce heat to medium and cook, stirring, for 3 to 5 minutes or until cooked to desired tenderness.

If desired, you can toast the pine nuts in a small skillet over medium-high heat, stirring, for 3 to 4 minutes or until just browned. Toasting adds depth of flavor to the nuts. Toast them in the large skillet, before starting step 1, to avoid dirtying an extra pan.

1 to 2 tbsp	extra virgin olive oil (see tip, page 108)	15 to 30 mL
4	chicken breast cutlets (about 1½ lbs/750 kg total)	4
3 tbsp	ghee (see tip, page 107)	45 mL
½ cup	dry white wine	125 mL
½ cup	ready-to-use reduced-sodium chicken broth	125 mL
1 tsp	dried basil	5 mL
1 tsp	paprika	5 mL
½ tsp	dried allspice	2 mL
3	yellow beets (see tip, at left), peeled and ends cut flat	3
1 cup	drained marinated artichoke hearts	250 mL
⅓ cup	Greek olives, pitted and halved	75 mL
2 tbsp	pine nuts (see tip, at left)	30 mL

1. In a large skillet, heat 1 tbsp (15 mL) oil over medium heat. Working in batches, add chicken and cook, turning once, for 3 to 5 minutes per side or until no longer pink inside, adding more oil and adjusting heat as necessary between batches. Transfer chicken to a plate and keep warm.

2. Melt ghee in the skillet, then add wine and broth, scraping up any browned bits from the bottom of the pan. Stir in basil, paprika and allspice; bring to a simmer.

3. Meanwhile, using a spiralizer, cut beets into medium strands. Add to skillet and cook, stirring, for 3 to 5 minutes or until cooked to desired tenderness. Using tongs, transfer beets to serving plates.

4. Return chicken and any accumulated juices to the skillet and stir in artichoke hearts and olives. Serve over beets, sprinkled with pine nuts.

Southern-Style Bourbon Chicken and Sweet Potatoes

If you are looking for a delectable Southern meal, you have found it here. The sweet and savory marinade makes the chicken incredibly tender and adds a golden-brown, rich glaze to the chicken and sweet potatoes.

MAKES 6 TO 8 SERVINGS

Tips

Water and vanilla replace traditional bourbon in this dish. If you would like to use bourbon, use ½ cup (125 mL) and omit the water and vanilla.

Buy the best-quality vanilla you can find and check the label to make sure it is pure vanilla without added sugars or non-paleo-friendly ingredients.

You can leave the skin on the sweet potato if you want to retain more of the nutrients and you enjoy eating the skin. You may need to add 1 to 3 minutes to the steaming time.

▶ **13- by 9-inch (33 by 23 cm) glass or ceramic baking dish**
▶ **Steamer basket**

6	cloves garlic, minced	6
1 tbsp	grated gingerroot	15 mL
1 tsp	kosher salt	5 mL
½ tsp	freshly ground black pepper	2 mL
½ cup	coconut amino acids	125 mL
6 tbsp	water	90 mL
⅓ cup	pure maple syrup or agave nectar	75 mL
3 tbsp	organic gluten-free vanilla extract	45 mL
3 tbsp	extra virgin olive oil (see tip, page 108)	45 mL
2½ lbs	chicken leg quarters	1.25 kg
6	small to medium sweet potatoes, peeled and ends cut flat	6

1. In baking dish, combine garlic, ginger, salt, pepper, coconut amino acids, water, maple syrup, vanilla and oil. Add chicken and turn to coat well. Cover and refrigerate for at least 8 hours or overnight.

2. Preheat oven to 425°F (220°C).

3. Uncover baking dish. Turn chicken to coat in marinade and arrange, skin side up, in a single layer. Bake for 45 to 60 minutes or until juices run clear when chicken is pierced.

4. Meanwhile, using a spiralizer, cut sweet potatoes into medium strands.

5. In a steamer basket set over a large saucepan of boiling water, steam sweet potatoes for 3 to 5 minutes or until cooked to desired tenderness.

6. Transfer sweet potatoes to a serving platter. Add chicken to platter. Skim off excess fat and pour sauce over sweet potatoes, if desired, or serve on the side.

Hungarian Chicken Paprikash with Wide Veggie Noodles

This classic dish has a rich, full-bodied flavor. While it is often served with the German pasta spaetzle or the Hungarian dumpling *halousky*, our version is served over sweet potato and celery root noodles.

Tips

Clarified butter contains virtually no lactose or milk proteins, so it doesn't cause the inflammation, sensitivities and intolerances that dairy products can. It is considered a healthy oil and has a high smoke point, so it is generally accepted in the paleo diet.

Conventional thinking is that dairy products are forbidden on the paleo diet; however, many followers feel that a moderate amount of dairy is not detrimental, particularly in the case of fermented milk products, such as sour cream and yogurt, which contain friendly bacteria that can improve digestion and gut health.

2	onions, peeled and ends cut flat	2
6 tbsp	clarified butter (see tip, at left), divided	90 mL
2 tbsp	paprika	30 mL
3 lbs	chicken legs and thighs	1.5 kg
2 cups	ready-to-use reduced-sodium chicken broth	500 mL
4	sweet potatoes, peeled and ends cut flat	4
1	celery root, peeled and ends cut flat	1
1 tbsp	extra virgin olive oil (see tip, page 108)	15 mL
¼ cup	sour cream or yogurt (see tip, at left)	60 mL
Pinch	kosher salt (optional)	Pinch
1½ to 2 tbsp	almond flour (optional)	22 mL to 30 mL

1. Using a spiralizer, cut onions into medium strands.
2. In a Dutch oven, melt 4 tbsp (60 mL) butter over medium-low heat. Stir in paprika. Add onions and cook, stirring, for 10 to 15 minutes or until lightly caramelized. Using a slotted spoon, transfer onions to a plate.
3. In the Dutch oven, melt 1 tbsp (15 mL) butter over medium heat. Working in batches, add chicken and cook, turning, for 7 to 9 minutes or until browned on all sides, adding more butter and adjusting heat as necessary between batches. Transfer chicken to a plate and keep warm.

Tip

Add other root vegetables, such as parsnips or turnips, either with the potatoes and celery root or in place of them. You will need about 6 cups (1.5 L) total of spiralized vegetables in any combination.

4. Return onions to the pot and stir in broth; reduce heat to medium-low, cover and simmer, stirring occasionally, for 45 to 60 minutes or until juices run clear when chicken is pierced.

5. Meanwhile, using a spiralizer, cut sweet potatoes and celery root into wide ribbons.

6. In a large skillet, heat oil over medium heat. Add sweet potatoes and celery root ribbons; cook, stirring, for 6 to 8 minutes or until cooked to desired tenderness.

7. Using tongs, transfer ribbons to a serving dish and top with chicken. Tent with foil to keep warm.

8. Add sour cream to the Dutch oven and stir well. Simmer over low heat for 3 to 5 minutes or until thickened. Season with salt (if using). If a thicker consistency is desired, stir in almond flour and simmer, stirring, until thickened. Pour gravy over chicken and ribbons. Serve immediately.

New World Kung Pao Chicken

A profusion of spicy, sweet, sour and salty flavors abound in this New World version of a classic Szechuan chicken and vegetable stir-fry. Served over parsnip noodles and topped with roasted peanuts, this dish is not to be missed.

**MAKES
2 SERVINGS**

Tips

Vinegar contains a very small amount of acetic acid, which can contribute to the net acid load in your diet; however, if you consume roughly one-third of your diet as vegetables and fruits, a little acid every once in a while should not be problematic.

Sesame oil is considered a healthy oil and is not inflammatory, so it is generally accepted in the paleo diet.

2 tsp	almond flour	10 mL
1 tsp	grated garlic	5 mL
¼ tsp	ground ginger	1 mL
¼ tsp	hot pepper flakes	1 mL
3 tbsp	water	45 mL
1½ tbsp	coconut amino acids	22 mL
1 tbsp	balsamic vinegar (see tip, at left)	15 mL
2 tsp	pure maple syrup or agave nectar	10 mL
1 tsp	orange juice	5 mL
½ tsp	almond butter	2 mL
8 oz	boneless skinless chicken thighs, cut into ½-inch (1 cm) pieces	250 g
2	parsnips, peeled and ends cut flat	2
2 tsp	sesame oil (see tip, at left), divided	10 mL
2	cloves garlic, minced	2
1 tsp	grated gingerroot	5 mL
½	red bell pepper, coarsely chopped	½
Pinch	kosher salt	Pinch
Pinch	freshly ground black pepper	Pinch
3	green onions, sliced diagonally	3
2 tbsp	crushed dry-roasted peanuts	30 mL

1. In a medium bowl, whisk together almond flour, grated garlic, ground ginger, hot pepper flakes, water, coconut amino acids, vinegar, maple syrup, orange juice and almond butter. Add chicken and stir to coat. Cover and refrigerate for 20 minutes.

2. Meanwhile, using a spiralizer, cut parsnips into medium strands. Set aside.

Tips

Do not overcook parsnip strands if you want to retain the noodle shape, as they can easily break apart.

If you would like your parsnip strands rice-shaped, after spiralizing, add the strands to a food processor and pulse a few times to the desired consistency.

3. In a large skillet, heat 1 tsp (5 mL) oil over medium-high heat. Using a slotted spoon, transfer chicken to skillet, reserving marinade, and cook, stirring, for 4 to 5 minutes or until browned and juices run clear when chicken is pierced. Transfer chicken to a plate and keep warm.

4. Reduce heat to medium and add the remaining oil to the skillet. Add minced garlic and grated ginger; cook, stirring, for 30 to 60 seconds or until garlic is lightly browned. Stir in red pepper, salt, black pepper and marinade; bring to a boil. Reduce heat and simmer, stirring, for 2 to 3 minutes or until thickened. Add parsnips and cook, tossing gently, for 3 to 5 minutes or until parsnips are cooked to desired tenderness and coated with sauce.

5. Return chicken and any accumulated juices to the pan and cook, tossing, for 1 minute. Serve sprinkled with green onions and peanuts.

Chinese Orange Chicken with Parsnip Noodles

Who needs takeout when you can make this classic Chinese dish right in your own kitchen. Enjoy the sweet, sour and savory flavors, knowing exactly what ingredients were used.

Tip

Choose parsnips that are firm, blemish-free and dry. Medium-size parsnips are often sweeter and firmer. Smaller parsnips tend to be softer, and larger ones can be over-ripened and woody.

8	parsnips, peeled and ends cut flat	8
1 lb	boneless skinless chicken thighs, cut into bite-size pieces	500 g
	Kosher salt	
	Freshly ground black pepper	
¼ cup	lard (approx.)	60 mL
2 tbsp	coconut flour	30 mL
½ tsp	ground ginger	2 mL
Pinch	hot pepper flakes (optional)	Pinch
1 cup	water	250 mL
	Grated zest of 1 orange	
½ cup	freshly squeezed orange juice	125 mL
3 tbsp	raw honey	45 mL
3 tbsp	coconut amino acids	45 mL
3	green onions, thinly sliced	3

1. Using a spiralizer, cut parsnips into thin strands. Set aside.

2. Season chicken with salt and pepper. In a large skillet, heat lard over medium-high heat. Add chicken and cook, stirring, for 5 to 7 minutes or until nicely browned and no longer pink inside. Transfer chicken to a plate and keep warm.

3. Reduce heat to medium. Add parsnips to skillet, adding more lard if necessary, and cook, stirring, for 5 to 7 minutes or until cooked to desired tenderness. Using tongs, transfer parsnips to a serving platter and keep warm. Drain any excess fat from the skillet.

Tip

If you would like your parsnip strands rice-shaped, after spiralizing, add the strands to a food processor and pulse a few times to the desired consistency. Omit step 3 and steam parsnip rice for 5 minutes.

4. Meanwhile, in a small saucepan, whisk together coconut flour, ginger, hot pepper flakes (if using), water, orange zest, orange juice, honey and coconut amino acids. Bring to a boil over medium-high heat. Reduce heat and simmer, stirring, for 5 to 7 minutes or until thickened.

5. Add chicken and half the orange sauce to the skillet, stirring to coat chicken in sauce.

6. Pour the remaining orange sauce over parsnips. Top with orange chicken and sprinkle with green onions.

General Tso's Chicken Zoodles

You will be delighted by this iconic Chinese-American dish that is slightly spicy and a bit sweet. Give it a unique twist by serving it over zucchini and broccoli noodles.

Tips

Arrowroot is a starch that has some acceptance in the paleo community if used in small amounts by individuals who can tolerate it. We have used it here to help the sauce coat the chicken and to thicken the sauce. While we feel it adds to the finished recipe, you can omit it.

Peeling broccoli stems makes them even on the outside and easier to spiralize.

When steaming vegetables, make sure they are set above the boiling water and do not touch the water.

› **Steamer basket**

1	small red chile pepper, finely minced	1
3 tsp	arrowroot (see tip, at left), divided	15 mL
½ cup	ready-to-use chicken broth	125 mL
2 tbsp	coconut amino acids	30 mL
1 tbsp	raw honey	15 mL
2 tsp	rice vinegar (see tip, opposite)	10 mL
4	zucchini, ends cut flat	4
1	large head broccoli, florets and stems separated	1
	Ice water	
1 lb	boneless skinless chicken thighs, cut into 1-inch (2.5 cm) pieces	500 g
Pinch	freshly ground black pepper	Pinch
2 tbsp	extra virgin olive oil (see tip, opposite), divided	30 mL
4	green onions, sliced	4
2	cloves garlic, minced	2
1 tsp	grated gingerroot	5 mL
2 tsp	toasted sesame seeds (optional)	10 mL

1. In a small bowl, whisk together chile, 1 tsp (5 mL) arrowroot, broth, coconut amino acids, honey and vinegar. Set aside.

2. Using a spiralizer, cut zucchini into thin strands. Peel broccoli stems and cut into thin strands, keeping them separate. Set aside.

3. In a steamer basket set over a saucepan of boiling water, steam broccoli florets for 2 to 4 minutes or until tender-crisp. Using a slotted spoon, immediately transfer broccoli to a bowl of ice water. Drain and set aside.

Tips

Vinegar contains a very small amount of acetic acid, which can contribute to the net acid load in your diet; however, if you consume roughly one-third of your diet as vegetables and fruits, a little acid every once in a while should not be problematic.

Extra virgin olive oil is considered a healthy oil and is not inflammatory, so it is generally accepted in the paleo diet.

4. Add zucchini to the steamer basket and steam for 2 to 3 minutes or until cooked to desired tenderness. Transfer zucchini to a colander to drain.

5. Place chicken in a medium bowl and add the remaining arrowroot and pepper, stirring to coat chicken evenly.

6. In a large skillet, heat $1\frac{1}{2}$ tbsp (22 mL) oil over medium-high heat. Add chicken and cook, stirring, for 7 to 9 minutes or until juices run clear when chicken is pierced. Transfer chicken to a plate.

7. Add the remaining oil to the skillet and reduce heat to medium. Add broccoli stem strands and cook, stirring, for 6 to 7 minutes or until cooked to desired tenderness. Using tongs, transfer strands to a serving bowl. Add zucchini strands and toss together. Set aside.

8. Add green onions, garlic and ginger to the skillet and cook, stirring, for 30 to 60 seconds or until lightly browned.

9. Return chicken and any accumulated juices to the pan and add broccoli florets; cook, stirring, for 2 to 3 minutes or until sauce is thickened and chicken and florets are coated with sauce. Serve over zucchini and broccoli strands. Sprinkle with sesame seeds, if desired.

Lettuce Wraps with Chicken, Grapes and Jicama

If you are looking for a lettuce wrap that has the right amount of crunch and a delectable package of sweet, spicy and savory, you will want to dive right in to this wrap.

Tips

If you refrigerate the filling for about 30 minutes at the end of step 2, the flavors will have a chance to meld together and deepen.

To make slicing grapes a breeze, lay them on a small plate. Turn another same-size plate upside down on top. Use a sharp knife to cut the grapes horizontally, between the plates.

2	carrots, peeled and ends cut flat	2
1	small jicama, peeled and ends cut flat	1
¼ cup	coconut amino acids	60 mL
2 tbsp	almond butter	30 mL
1 tsp	minced garlic	5 mL
½ tsp	hot pepper flakes	2 mL
Pinch	freshly ground black pepper	Pinch
1 tbsp	raw honey	15 mL
2 tsp	cider vinegar (see tip, page 114)	10 mL
2 tsp	sesame oil (see tip, page 114)	10 mL
3 cups	shredded cooked chicken (preferably rotisserie)	750 mL
1 cup	seedless grapes, halved	250 mL
1	stalk celery, chopped	1
½	onion, chopped	½
12	leaves iceberg lettuce	12

1. Using a spiralizer, cut carrots and jicama into medium strands. Pat jicama strands dry. Set aside.

2. In a large bowl, using a fork, combine coconut amino acids and almond butter until a paste forms. Stir in garlic, hot pepper flakes, black pepper, honey, vinegar and oil until smooth. Add carrots, jicama, chicken, grapes, celery and onion, tossing to coat.

3. Lay 2 lettuce leaves on each of six plates and place one-twelfth of the chicken filling on each leaf. Wrap the lettuce leaves around the filling.

Leftover Turkey Tetrazzini

You have served your big holiday turkey dinner and are tired of eating turkey sandwiches, so now it's time to try something new with that leftover turkey. This tetrazzini fits the bill and is extremely satisfying.

**MAKES
6 SERVINGS**

Tips

Clarified butter contains virtually no lactose or milk proteins, so it doesn't cause the inflammation, sensitivities and intolerances that dairy products can. It is considered a healthy oil and has a high smoke point, so it is generally accepted in the paleo diet.

Your sauce should be very thick, with no runny liquids at all. The zucchini strands will release water when they are baked, so your sauce will get more watery.

Paleo Parmesan (see tip, page 123) can be substituted for the nutritional yeast.

▶ **Preheat oven to 375°F (190°C)**
▶ **13- by 9-inch (33 by 23 cm) glass baking dish**

8	small zucchini, ends cut flat	8
2 tbsp	clarified butter (see tip, at left)	30 mL
8 oz	mushrooms, sliced	250 g
1/2 cup	chopped onion	125 mL
4	cloves garlic, minced	4
2 tsp	dried thyme	10 mL
1 tsp	kosher salt	5 mL
1 tsp	freshly ground black pepper	5 mL
1/2 cup	ready-to-use chicken broth	125 mL
1/2 cup	almond milk	125 mL
2 tbsp	arrowroot (optional; see tip, page 118)	30 mL
2 cups	cubed cooked turkey	500 mL
1/2 cup	nutritional yeast	125 mL

1. Using a spiralizer, cut zucchini into medium strands. Set aside.

2. In a large skillet, melt butter over medium heat. Add mushrooms and onion; cook, stirring, for 5 to 7 minutes or until onions are translucent and liquid is absorbed. Add garlic and cook, stirring, for 30 seconds.

3. Stir in thyme, salt, pepper, broth and almond milk; bring to a simmer. Reduce heat and simmer, stirring, for 5 to 7 minutes or until sauce is thickened (see tip, at left). If a thicker sauce is desired, stir in arrowroot, a little bit at a time. Stir in turkey and remove from heat.

4. Add zucchini and toss to combine ingredients and coat noodles. Pour into baking dish and sprinkle with nutritional yeast.

5. Bake in preheated oven for 25 to 30 minutes or until top is golden brown and edges are bubbling. Let cool slightly before cutting.

Beef Bolognese with Zucchini Noodles

Everyone will enjoy this easy, comforting dish. It tastes just as fabulous as traditional pasta, without that overstuffed feeling.

MAKES 4 SERVINGS

Tip

To peel and crush tomatoes, bring a large pot of water to a rolling boil and prepare a large bowl of ice water. Cut a 1½-inch (4 cm) slit in each tomato. Working in batches, add tomatoes to the pot and cook for 30 seconds. Using a slotted spoon, immediately transfer tomatoes to the ice water. Let cool. Using your fingers, peel off the tomato skins. Cut tomatoes into wedges and transfer to a large bowl. Crush tomatoes with a wire potato masher (which is also handy for breaking up ground beef quickly and easily while it's cooking).

1 lb	lean ground beef	500 g
2 tbsp	extra virgin olive oil (see tip, page 124), divided	30 mL
8 oz	mushrooms, sliced	250 g
1	onion, peeled and ends cut flat	1
4	cloves garlic, minced	4
4 cups	crushed peeled tomatoes (about 3½ lbs/1.75 kg)	1 L
¼ cup	minced reconstituted sun-dried tomatoes	60 mL
1 tsp	dried basil	5 mL
1 tsp	dried oregano	5 mL
½ tsp	dried thyme	2 mL
6	zucchini, ends cut flat	6
½ cup	Paleo Parmesan (optional; see tip, opposite)	125 mL
	Hot pepper flakes (optional)	

1. In a large saucepan, cook beef over medium-high heat, breaking it up with a spoon, for 7 to 9 minutes or until no longer pink. Using a slotted spoon, transfer beef to a plate. Drain off fat from pan.

2. Reduce heat to medium and heat 1 tbsp (15 mL) oil in the saucepan. Add mushrooms and onion; cook, stirring, for 5 to 7 minutes or until mushrooms have released their liquid and are starting to brown. Add garlic and cook, stirring, for 30 to 60 seconds or until fragrant.

Tips

To make ½ cup (125 mL) Paleo Parmesan, a replacement for Parmesan cheese, in a food processor, process ½ cup (125 mL) whole raw almonds, 2 tbsp (30 mL) nutritional yeast and ¼ tsp (1 mL) kosher salt until fluffy and no chunks of nuts remain.

Cook your sauce slightly thicker than you would for a traditional pasta dish. The zucchini will add liquid to it.

3. Return beef and any accumulated juices to the pan and stir in crushed tomatoes, sun-dried tomatoes, basil, oregano and thyme; bring to a gentle boil. Reduce heat to low, cover and simmer, stirring occasionally, for 30 to 40 minutes or until sauce is desired thickness (see tip at left).

4. Meanwhile, using a spiralizer, cut zucchini into thin strands.

5. In a medium skillet, heat the remaining oil over medium heat. Add zucchini and cook, tossing gently, for 3 to 5 minutes or until cooked to desired tenderness.

6. Using tongs, transfer zucchini to individual serving plates. Top with sauce. If desired, garnish with Paleo Parmesan and hot pepper flakes.

Carnitas and Plantain Noodles with Grilled Pineapple Salsa

Carnitas means "little meats" in Spanish, but there's nothing little about the flavors in this slow-braised pork roast. Sweet pineapple and the heat from the peppers dance with curly plantain noodles and melt-in-your-mouth pork.

MAKES 6 TO 8 SERVINGS

Tips

Extra virgin olive oil and sesame oil are considered healthy oils and are not inflammatory, so they are generally accepted in the paleo diet.

You may need to cut the pork roast into sections to fit it into the Dutch oven.

▸ **Preheat oven to 350°F (180°C)**
▸ **Grill pan or barbecue grill**

Salsa

3	slices fresh pineapple (½ inch/ 1 cm thick)	3
3 tbsp	extra virgin olive oil (see tip, at left)	45 mL
1	small red onion, finely chopped	1
1	jalapeño pepper, minced	1
½ cup	chopped fresh cilantro	125 mL
1 tsp	kosher salt	5 mL
3 tbsp	freshly squeezed lime juice	45 mL

Carnitas

2 lb	boneless pork shoulder blade roast	1 kg
2 tsp	kosher salt	10 mL
1 tsp	freshly ground black pepper	5 mL
¼ cup	olive oil	60 mL
2	cloves garlic, minced	2
1	onion, finely chopped	1
1½ cups	ready-to-use reduced-sodium chicken broth	375 mL
1 tbsp	dried oregano	15 mL
	Grated zest and juice of 1 lemon	
	Grated zest and juice of 1 lime	

Plantains

8 oz	thick-cut sliced bacon	250 g
5	unripe plantains, peeled and ends cut flat	5
2 tbsp	sesame oil	30 mL
1 tbsp	chopped garlic	15 mL
Pinch	freshly ground black pepper	Pinch

Tips

Choose large plantains that are green (unripened) and relatively straight. Green plantains are firmer and work better in the spiralizer. If the strands break into smaller strands, that is fine.

Leftover pineapple salsa will keep in the refrigerator for 1 to 2 days.

1. *Salsa:* Preheat grill pan or barbecue grill over medium heat. Brush pineapple with olive oil, reserving the remaining oil. Grill pineapple, turning once, for 5 to 7 minutes or until browned and tender. Let cool, then dice.

2. In a small bowl, combine pineapple, onion, jalapeño, cilantro, salt, lime juice and the remaining olive oil. Cover and refrigerate until ready to serve.

3. *Carnitas:* Season pork with salt and pepper. In a Dutch oven, heat olive oil over medium-high heat. Add pork and cook, turning often, for 10 to 12 minutes or until browned on all sides. Transfer pork to a bowl and drain off all but 2 tbsp (30 mL) of the fat from the pot.

4. Add garlic and onion to the fat remaining in the pot and cook over medium-low heat, stirring, for 2 to 3 minutes or until just softened. Add broth, scraping up any browned bits from the bottom of the pot.

5. Return pork and any accumulated juices to the pot and add oregano, lemon zest, lemon juice, lime zest and lime juice. Cover, reduce heat to low and simmer for $2\frac{1}{2}$ to 3 hours or until roast is fork-tender. Transfer roast to a cutting board, cover with foil and let rest for 10 minutes, then cut into cubes, trimming off excess fat. Keep hot.

6. *Plantains:* In a large skillet, cook bacon over medium heat until crisp. Transfer bacon to a plate lined with paper towels and drain off all but 1 tbsp (15 mL) fat from the pan. Let bacon cool, then crumble into medium pieces.

7. Meanwhile, using a spiralizer, cut plantains into medium strands.

8. Add sesame oil to the fat remaining in the skillet and heat over medium-low heat. Add plantains and garlic; cook, stirring, for 3 to 5 minutes or until plantains are golden brown. Remove from heat and stir in bacon and pepper. Serve with roasted pork and pineapple salsa.

Pork Sugo with Rutabaga Noodles

Sugo means "sauce" in Italian, and this make-ahead dish features an aromatic, flavorful sauce that harmonizes perfectly with the tender pork and the sweet and savory rutabagas.

~~~

MAKES 10 TO 12 SERVINGS

Tips

You may need to cut the pork roast into sections to fit it into the Dutch oven.

Vinegar contains a very small amount of acetic acid, which can contribute to the net acid load in your diet; however, if you consume roughly one-third of your diet as vegetables and fruits, a little acid every once in a while should not be problematic.

To make 1 cup (250 mL) Paleo Parmesan, a replacement for Parmesan cheese, in a food processor, process 1 cup (250 mL) whole raw almonds, ¼ cup (60 mL) nutritional yeast and ½ tsp (2 mL) kosher salt until fluffy and no chunks of nuts remain.

▷ **Preheat oven to 325°F (160°C)**
▷ **Ovenproof Dutch oven**

3 lb	boneless pork shoulder blade roast (see tip, at left)	1.5 kg
1 tbsp	kosher salt	15 mL
2 tsp	freshly ground black pepper	10 mL
3 tbsp	extra virgin olive oil (see tip, page 119)	45 mL
4	onions, peeled and ends cut flat	4
2	carrots, peeled and ends cut flat	2
1 cup	chopped celery	250 mL
3	cloves garlic, minced	3
5	fresh sage leaves, chopped	5
2	sprigs fresh rosemary leaves	2
¼ cup	minced reconstituted sun-dried tomatoes	60 mL
1 cup	white wine vinegar (see tip, at left)	250 mL
5 cups	ready-to-use reduced-sodium chicken broth, divided	1.25 L
5	rutabagas, peeled and ends cut flat	5
1 tsp	chopped fresh parsley	5 mL
1 cup	Paleo Parmesan (see tip, at left), divided	250 mL
Pinch	hot pepper flakes (optional)	Pinch

1. Season pork with salt and pepper. In a Dutch oven, heat oil over medium-high heat. Add pork and cook, turning, for 10 to 12 minutes or until browned on all sides.

2. Cover Dutch oven tightly and roast in preheated oven for 2 hours. Turn pork and roast, uncovered, for 1 to 2 hours or until pork pulls apart easily. Transfer roast to a cutting board, cover with foil and let rest for 10 minutes, then shred, discarding excess fat.

Tips

Pork sugo can be made ahead through step 6. Let cool, cover and refrigerate for up to 24 hours. Wait to spiralize the rutabagas until you are ready to complete the dish, and reheat the pork sugo for 9 to 12 minutes or until heated through, while you're spiralizing.

If you have a fattier pork roast or just want to reduce the amount of fat, after step 2 you can refrigerate the roasted pork overnight, then remove any congealed fat before proceeding with step 3.

3. Using a spiralizer, cut onions into medium strands and carrots into wide ribbons, keeping them separate.

4. Remove all but 3 tbsp (45 mL) fat from the Dutch oven. Heat the remaining fat over medium heat. Add onion strands and celery; cook, stirring, for 5 to 7 minutes or until onions are translucent. Add carrot ribbons, garlic, sage and rosemary; cook, stirring, for about 1 minute or until garlic is fragrant. Add tomatoes and cook, stirring, for 3 minutes.

5. Add vinegar, scraping up any browned bits from the bottom of the pot. Reduce heat and simmer, stirring, for 5 to 7 minutes or until liquid is reduced by half.

6. Stir in shredded pork and 4 cups (1 L) broth; simmer, stirring occasionally, for 30 minutes or until sauce is thickened.

7. Meanwhile, using a spiralizer, cut rutabagas into wide ribbons.

8. Add rutabaga and the remaining broth to the pot and simmer for 5 to 7 minutes or until rutabaga is cooked to desired tenderness. Stir in half the Paleo Parmesan and the hot pepper flakes (if using). Serve immediately, garnished with the remaining Paleo Parmesan.

Mojo Pork with Sweet Potato Noodles

This dish's pleasant and distinctive aroma will have your taste buds watering, and the anticipation will be rewarded with the flavorful combination of mojo rub, tangy citrus and sweet potatoes.

MAKES 4 SERVINGS

Tip

You can use a meat thermometer inserted horizontally into the chops (without touching bone) to check the internal temperature of the pork chops, if desired. For medium-well, remove the chops from the heat when the temperature reaches 155°F (68°C). The meat will rise about 5°F (3°C) as it rests.

Mojo Rub

8	cloves garlic, minced	8
1 tbsp	dried onion flakes	15 mL
½ tsp	dried oregano	2 mL
½ tsp	ground cumin	2 mL
½ tsp	kosher salt	2 mL
½ tsp	freshly ground black pepper	2 mL

Sweet Potatoes and Pork

6	sweet potatoes, peeled and ends cut flat	6
1	large onion, peeled and ends cut flat	1
4	bone-in pork chops (about 1 inch/2.5 cm thick)	4
4 tbsp	virgin coconut oil (see tip, opposite), divided	60 mL
1	clove garlic, minced	1
⅓ cup	freshly squeezed orange juice	75 mL
⅓ cup	freshly squeezed lime juice	75 mL
2 tbsp	chopped fresh cilantro	30 mL

1. *Mojo Rub:* In a small bowl, combine garlic, onion flakes, oregano, cumin, salt and pepper. Set aside.

2. *Sweet Potatoes and Pork:* Using a spiralizer, cut sweet potatoes and onion into medium strands, keeping them separate. Set aside.

Coconut oil is considered a healthy oil and as such is generally accepted in the paleo diet. It works well with the character of this recipe.

3. Rub pork chops with mojo rub, reserving any remaining rub. In a large skillet, heat 2 tbsp (30 mL) coconut oil over medium-high heat. Add pork and sear both sides. Reduce heat to medium and cook, turning once, for 7 to 9 minutes or until just a hint of pink remains in pork. Transfer to a warm plate and tent with foil to keep warm.

4. In the same skillet, melt the remaining coconut oil over medium heat. Add onion strands and cook, stirring, for 5 to 7 minutes or until translucent. Add garlic and cook, stirring, for 30 seconds or until fragrant.

5. Stir in orange juice, lime juice and any remaining rub. Add sweet potatoes and cook, stirring, for 3 to 5 minutes or until not quite tender. Gently stir in cilantro and top with chops. Cover and heat for 2 to 3 minutes or until sweet potatoes are cooked to desired tenderness.

Pork and Zucchini Noodle Bowls

If you love spring rolls, you will truly enjoy this robust Asian-inspired dish — it is reminiscent of spring rolls, but without any rolling!

MAKES 4 SERVINGS

Tips

Choose zucchini that are straight and fairly even in diameter. This will make it easier to spiral-cut them evenly.

Choose carrots that are as straight as you can find to make it easier to cut them in your spiralizer. Thicker carrots work best, but choose those that are just large, not overgrown. Older, overgrown carrots take on a woody flavor.

You can use the spiralizer to cut the onion, too. The medium blade works best here. You can then finely chop the strands or just cut them into smaller lengths.

3	zucchini, ends cut flat	3
1	large carrot, peeled and ends cut flat	1
1 lb	ground pork	500 g
1 tbsp	extra virgin olive oil (see tip, opposite)	15 mL
2	cloves garlic, minced	2
1	small onion, finely chopped	1
1	red bell pepper, finely chopped	1
1 tsp	hot pepper flakes	5 mL
Pinch	kosher salt	Pinch
Pinch	freshly ground black pepper	Pinch
1	can (14 oz/400 mL) coconut milk	1
1/2 cup	cashew butter or other nut butter	125 mL
1/4 cup	coconut amino acids	60 mL
3 tbsp	hot pepper sauce (such as Sriracha)	45 mL
2 tbsp	freshly squeezed lime juice	30 mL
2 tbsp	chopped fresh cilantro	30 mL
2/3 cup	bean sprouts (optional)	150 mL

1. Using a spiralizer, cut zucchini and carrot into thin strands, keeping them separate. Set aside.

2. In a medium skillet, cook pork over medium-high heat, breaking it up with a spoon, for 7 to 9 minutes or until no longer pink. Using a slotted spoon, transfer pork to a plate. Drain off fat from pan.

Tips

If you have a leftover pork roast, shred the pork to yield 1½ cups (375 mL). Use it instead of the ground pork and skip step 2.

Extra virgin olive oil is considered a healthy oil and is not inflammatory, so it is generally accepted in the paleo diet.

3. Reduce heat to medium and add oil, garlic, onion, red pepper, hot pepper flakes, salt and black pepper to the skillet. Cook, stirring, for 5 to 7 minutes or until onion and red pepper are softened. Add carrot strands and sauté for 3 minutes.

4. Return pork and any accumulated juices to the pan and add zucchini; cook, stirring, for 2 to 3 minutes or until carrot and zucchini are cooked to desired tenderness. Remove from heat and divide among four serving bowls.

5. Meanwhile, in a small saucepan over medium heat, whisk together coconut milk, cashew butter, coconut amino acids, hot pepper sauce and lime juice. Reduce heat to low and cook, stirring, for 5 to 7 minutes or until sauce is thickened to your desired consistency.

6. Pour sauce over pork and vegetables and toss to combine. Sprinkle with cilantro. Top with bean sprouts (if using).

Hungarian Pork Stew with Kohlrabi Noodles

This mouthwatering pork stew is typically served with tiny little dumplings called spaetzle, made of flour and eggs. Our version uses spiralized kohlrabi, a favorite European vegetable, giving it a hearty, gluten-free twist.

MAKES 8 TO 10 SERVINGS

Tips

You can substitute ground caraway seeds for whole, but reduce the amount to 1 tsp (5 mL).

Choose kohlrabi that feel heavy for their size. Lighter kohlrabi are over-ripened, can be woody inside and will not be as crisp and sweet.

Kohlrabi leaves can also be eaten. They are delightful mixed in with other greens or seasoned and boiled as a side dish.

2 lb	boneless pork shoulder blade roast, cut into 1½-inch (4 cm) cubes	1 kg
1 tbsp	kosher salt	15 mL
2 tsp	freshly ground black pepper	10 mL
½ cup	extra virgin olive oil (see tip, page 131), divided	125 mL
8	onions, finely chopped	8
3	cloves garlic, minced	3
	Water	
3 tbsp	Hungarian paprika	45 mL
1 tbsp	caraway seeds	15 mL
2 tsp	almond flour (optional)	10 mL
10	kohlrabi, peeled and ends cut flat	10

1. Season pork with salt and pepper. In a large skillet, heat 3 tbsp (45 mL) oil over medium-high heat. Add pork and cook, stirring, for 3 to 5 minutes or until white on all sides. Reduce heat to medium and add onions and garlic; cook, stirring, until onions are softened.

2. Add enough water to reach 1 inch (2.5 cm) up the skillet; increase heat to high and bring to a boil. Reduce heat to medium-low, cover and simmer, stirring occasionally and adding water as necessary, for 45 to 60 minutes or until pork is fork-tender. Stir in paprika and caraway seeds. If a thicker consistency is desired, stir in almond flour and simmer, stirring, until thickened. Reduce heat to low and keep warm.

3. Meanwhile, using a spiralizer, cut kohlrabi into medium strands.

4. In another large skillet, heat the remaining oil over medium heat. Add kohlrabi and cook, stirring, for 6 to 8 minutes or until cooked to desired tenderness.

5. Transfer kohlrabi strands to a serving plate and top with stew.

Vegetarian and Vegan Recipes

Crunchy Cashew Slaw

There is so much going on in this easy-to-make salad you will never get tired of it. Creamy, crunchy and packed with flavor, this slaw is a company-worthy dish.

Tips

Wear gloves when working with red beets so they don't stain your hands. Wash your spiralizer immediately after cutting beets to avoid discoloration.

The dressing can be stored in an airtight container in the refrigerator for up to 3 days.

2	carrots, peeled and ends cut flat	2
1	head green cabbage, outer leaves removed, cut in half and ends cut flat	1
1	red beet, peeled and ends cut flat	1
5	green onions, sliced diagonally	5
1 cup	cooked shelled edamame	250 mL
¼ cup	virgin coconut oil, melted	60 mL
2 tbsp	freshly squeezed lime juice	30 mL
2 tbsp	soy sauce or tamari	30 mL
1 tbsp	pure maple syrup	15 mL
1 tbsp	rice vinegar	15 mL
1 tbsp	stone-ground mustard	15 mL
1 tbsp	sesame oil	15 mL
	Kosher salt	
	Freshly ground black pepper	
1 cup	unsalted roasted cashews	250 mL
½ cup	dried cranberries	125 mL

1. Using a spiralizer, cut carrots, cabbage and beet into medium strands. Trim all strands into 3-inch (7.5 cm) lengths.

2. In a large bowl, toss carrot, cabbage and beet strands with green onions and edamame.

3. In a small bowl, whisk together coconut oil, lime juice, soy sauce, maple syrup, vinegar, mustard and sesame oil. Season to taste with salt and pepper.

4. Pour dressing over cabbage mixture and toss to combine. Gently toss in cashews and cranberries.

Twisted Thai Salad with Peanut Lime Dressing

A bounty of vegetables is topped by a sassy peanut lime dressing that will awaken your taste buds.

MAKES 6 TO 8 SERVINGS

Tips

When spiralizing, you always end up with a little bit of vegetable or fruit that is too small to spiralize. I use these pieces to taste-test my dressing before adding it to the salad.

The dressing doubles easily and can be stored in an airtight container in the refrigerator for up to 3 days. It's delicious on a variety of salads or as a dipping sauce for tofu satay.

▶ **Food processor or blender**

3	carrots, peeled and ends cut flat	3
3	yellow beets, peeled and ends cut flat	3
1	jicama, peeled and ends cut flat	1
1	small cucumber, ends cut flat	1
½	small head green cabbage, outer leaves peeled and ends cut flat	½
1	clove garlic, coarsely chopped	1
5 tbsp	peanuts, divided	75 mL
¼ cup	peanut oil	60 mL
1½ tsp	peanut butter	7 mL
1 tsp	liquid honey	5 mL
1 tsp	tamari or soy sauce	5 mL
	Grated zest and juice of 2 limes	
3 tbsp	chopped fresh cilantro	45 mL

1. Using a spiralizer, cut carrots, beets and jicama into thin strands. Pat jicama strands dry. Cut cucumber and cabbage into wide ribbons. Pat cucumber ribbons dry. Trim all strands and ribbons to 4-inch (10 cm) lengths. Toss together in a large serving bowl.

2. In food processor, combine garlic, 3 tbsp (45 mL) peanuts, peanut oil, peanut butter, honey, tamari, lime zest and lime juice; process until almost smooth and only a few chunks remain.

3. Drizzle dressing on top of salad. Garnish with cilantro and the remaining peanuts.

Curly Beet and Crispy Sweet Onion Salad with Horseradish Cream

This salad makes an ideal side dish for a variety of entrées. The delicate horseradish cream sauce highlights the earthy taste of beets and crispy sweet onion twirls to make a tasty and eye-catching presentation.

MAKES 4 SERVINGS

Tips

Beet colors vary from yellow to deep red. Choose the best of the season each time you make this salad, or mix different colors for added interest.

Prepared horseradish can be found in the refrigerated section of your grocer. Horseradish sauce will not yield the same results.

▸ **Preheat oven to 425°F (220°C), with one rack in the upper third and one in the bottom third**
▸ **2 rimmed baking sheets, lined with foil**

4	beets, peeled and ends cut flat	4
3 tbsp	olive oil, divided	45 mL
	Kosher salt	
1	sweet onion (such as Vidalia or Walla Walla), peeled and ends cut flat	1
	Seasoned salt	
¼ cup	crème fraîche	60 mL
2 tsp	prepared horseradish	10 mL
¼ cup	chopped walnuts	60 mL
	Freshly cracked black pepper (optional)	

1. Using a spiralizer, cut beets into wide ribbons. Place beets on a prepared baking sheet, drizzle with 2 tbsp (30 mL) oil and season with kosher salt. Toss to coat, then separate ribbons so they are not touching.

2. Cut onion into medium strands. Place on the other prepared baking sheet, drizzle with the remaining oil and season with seasoned salt. Toss to coat, then separate strands so they are not touching.

3. Place onions on lower rack in oven and bake, tossing occasionally, for 10 minutes. Add beets to the upper rack and bake, tossing once, for 5 to 10 minutes or until onions are crispy but not burned and beets are cooked to desired tenderness.

4. Meanwhile, in a small bowl, combine crème fraîche and horseradish.

5. Transfer beets to individual serving plates. Top with crispy onions. Drizzle with horseradish crème. Sprinkle with walnuts and pepper to taste (if using).

The Ultimate Spiralized Greek Salad

The kiss of the Mediterranean sun is yours with a bounty of fresh vegetables, kalamata olives and a quintessential Greek vinaigrette.

Tips

After spiralizing bell peppers, you will need to remove the white flesh and seeds from the strands. Alternatively, you can core the peppers, but they will not hold their shape as well during spiralizing.

If available, use sun-ripened tomatoes in this salad.

Vegan Feta: In a food processor, process 1 cup (250 mL) raw cashews, 2 tbsp (30 mL) extra virgin olive oil, 1 tbsp (15 mL) dried oregano and a pinch of kosher salt; process to a consistency similar to crumbled feta.

2	cucumbers, ends cut flat	2
1	small red onion, peeled and ends cut flat	1
1	small green bell pepper, stem removed (see tip, at left)	1
1	small yellow bell pepper, stem removed	1
4	tomatoes, cored and cut into sixths	4
1 cup	kalamata olives, pitted	250 mL
¼ cup	torn fresh parsley (optional)	60 mL
2	cloves garlic, minced	2
1 tbsp	chopped fresh oregano	15 mL
½ cup	extra virgin olive oil	125 mL
¼ cup	red wine vinegar	60 mL
	Kosher salt	
	Freshly ground black pepper	
¾ cup	crumbled feta cheese or Vegan Feta (see tip, at left)	175 mL

1. Using a spiralizer, cut cucumbers into wide ribbons and pat dry. Cut onion, green pepper and yellow pepper into medium strands. Remove white flesh and seeds from peppers. Trim all ribbons and strands to desired lengths.

2. In a large bowl, combine spiralized vegetables, tomatoes, olives and parsley (if using).

3. In a small bowl, whisk together garlic, oregano, oil and vinegar. Season to taste with salt and pepper.

4. Pour dressing over salad and toss to combine. Sprinkle cheese over top.

Spinach, Quinoa and Curly Apple Salad with Pecans and Cranberries

Spinach salad gets a new twist with spiral-cut apples and flavorful toppings. The elegant results come together in minutes.

**MAKES
4 SERVINGS**

Tips

You will need ¼ cup (60 mL) quinoa to yield 1 cup (250 mL) cooked.

I recommend using full-fat yogurt in this recipe because it is less processed and recent studies have shown the superior health benefits of full-fat dairy. If you prefer low-fat yogurt, you can use that as a substitute in this recipe.

½ tsp	kosher salt	2 mL
¼ tsp	freshly ground black pepper	1 mL
½ cup	plain yogurt (see tip, at left)	125 mL
2 tbsp	cider vinegar	30 mL
1 tsp	Dijon mustard	5 mL
1 tsp	liquid honey	5 mL
4	crisp apples, cored	4
1	small red onion, peeled and ends cut flat	1
1 cup	cooked quinoa, cooled (see tip, at left)	250 mL
½ cup	chopped pecans	125 mL
⅓ cup	dried cranberries	75 mL
6 cups	baby spinach	1.5 L
½ cup	crumbled feta cheese (optional)	125 mL

1. In a jar with a tight-fitting lid, combine salt, pepper, yogurt, vinegar, mustard and honey. Cover tightly and shake vigorously to combine. Set aside.

2. Using a spiralizer, cut apples and onion into medium strands.

3. In a large bowl, combine apples, onion, quinoa, pecans and cranberries. Add dressing and toss to combine. Cover and refrigerate for 20 minutes.

4. Place spinach in a large serving bowl. Top with quinoa mixture. Sprinkle with cheese (if using).

Variation

Substitute 1 cup (250 mL) rinsed drained canned chickpeas for the quinoa.

Curried Chickpea and Veggie Salad

A bounty of fresh vegetables awaits you in this gloriously colorful and delicious salad with a hint of Indian-inspired flavors. Plus, it's both vegan and gluten-free!

Tips

Choose carrots that are as straight as you can find to make it easier to cut them in your spiralizer. Thicker carrots work best, but choose those that are just large, not overgrown. Older, overgrown carrots take on a woody flavor.

Choose zucchini that are straight and fairly even in diameter. This will make it easier to spiral-cut them evenly.

1 tsp	curry powder	5 mL
½ tsp	freshly ground black pepper	2 mL
Pinch	kosher salt	Pinch
¼ cup	grapeseed oil	60 mL
2 tbsp	white wine vinegar	30 mL
2 tsp	pure maple syrup	10 mL
2	carrots, peeled and ends cut flat	2
2	zucchini, ends cut flat	2
3	green onions, sliced	3
2 cups	loosely packed arugula	500 mL
1 cup	rinsed drained canned chickpeas	250 mL
¼ cup	packed fresh cilantro, chopped	60 mL

1. In a small bowl, combine curry powder, pepper, salt, oil, vinegar and maple syrup. Set aside.
2. Using a spiralizer, cut carrots and zucchini into thin strands.
3. In a large serving bowl, combine carrots, zucchini, green onions, arugula, chickpeas and cilantro. Add dressing and toss to coat.

Variations

Light (fancy) molasses is a nice substitute for the maple syrup (for a vegan dressing), or you can substitute honey (for a vegetarian dressing).

For a creamier, nutty dressing, reduce the grapeseed oil to 2 tbsp (30 mL) and add 2 tbsp (30 mL) tahini.

Vietnamese-Inspired Vegetarian Salad

This Vietnamese-style dish, called *gòi chay* in many homes and restaurants, is as varied as the culture and topography of Vietnam. While it's often made with tofu or meat, chickpeas anchor my version of this flavorful dish.

Tips

While wonderful by itself, this dish can also be served over cooked rice noodles or raw zucchini noodles (use 4 zucchini and cut them into medium strands).

If you like more heat in your dressing, add the seeds from the chile pepper.

1	clove garlic, minced	1
1	medium-low-heat chile pepper (such as serrano or jalapeño), seeded and finely chopped	1
¼ cup	freshly squeezed lemon juice	60 mL
2 tbsp	soy sauce	30 mL
2	carrots, peeled and ends cut flat	2
1	head green cabbage, outer leaves removed, cut in half and ends cut flat	1
1½ tbsp	chopped fresh basil	22 mL
1 tbsp	chopped fresh cilantro	15 mL
2 tsp	chopped fresh mint	10 mL
1	can (14 oz/398 mL) chickpeas, drained and rinsed	1
½ cup	unsalted roasted peanuts, finely chopped	125 mL
4 oz	bean sprouts	125 g

1. In a small bowl, combine garlic, chile, lemon juice and soy sauce. Set aside.

2. Using a spiralizer, cut carrots and cabbage into medium strands.

3. In a large bowl, combine carrots, cabbage, basil, cilantro, mint and chickpeas. Add dressing and toss to combine. Let stand for 15 minutes to blend the flavors, or cover and refrigerate for up to 1 day. Sprinkle with peanuts and bean sprouts just before serving.

Yellow Beet, Fennel and White Bean Winter Salad

Here, crispy, subtle, licorice-scented fennel complements beets and white beans while a mint-orange vinaigrette ties it all together.

Tip

I like cooking the fennel strands because it softens them a bit, but if you like a crunchier texture, you can eliminate part of step 2. You will still need to cook the beets for 2 to 3 minutes more.

2	yellow beets, peeled and ends cut flat	2
1	fennel bulb, tops trimmed, ends cut flat	1
3 tbsp	olive oil	45 mL
2	cloves garlic, minced	2
1 tbsp	chopped fresh mint	15 mL
3 tbsp	grapeseed oil	45 mL
2 tbsp	orange juice	30 mL
1 tbsp	cider vinegar	15 mL
1	can (14 oz/398 mL) white beans, drained and rinsed	1
	Kosher salt	
	Freshly ground black pepper	
3 oz	pecorino cheese, shaved	90 g

1. Using a spiralizer, cut beets into medium strands. Cut fennel bulb into fine strands, keeping them separate, and trim to 3-inch (7.5 cm) lengths. Set aside.

2. In a large skillet, heat olive oil over medium heat. Add beets and garlic; cook, stirring, for 3 minutes. Add fennel and cook, stirring, for 2 to 3 minutes or until beets are cooked to desired tenderness and fennel is still firm. Let cool.

3. In a small bowl, whisk together mint, grapeseed oil, orange juice and vinegar.

4. In a large bowl, combine beet mixture and beans. Add dressing and toss to coat. Season to taste with salt and pepper. Garnish with cheese.

Variations

Use 2 small kohlrabi instead of the beets.

Twisted Beet, Fennel, Orange and Olive Salad: Peel and pit 1 navel orange, remove the pith and slice the orange crosswise. Before garnishing the salad with cheese, top it with orange slices and $1/2$ cup (125 mL) sliced black olives.

Tex-Mex Zucchini Salad with Zesty Lime Dressing

A symphony of textures and flavors bursts from this sensational combination of ingredients. The zesty lime dressing brings out all the notes while allowing the full concert to soar.

MAKES 3 TO 4 SERVINGS

Tips

For a pretty presentation, layer the salad ingredients one by one in a clear glass serving bowl, such as a trifle bowl.

Top the salad with sliced black olives, sliced jalapeño peppers and/or hot pepper flakes for added variety.

2	zucchini, ends cut flat	2
2	carrots, peeled and ends cut flat	2
8 oz	cherry tomatoes, cut in half	250 g
1	can (14 oz/398 mL) black beans, drained and rinsed	1
1	clove garlic, minced	1
1 tbsp	chopped fresh cilantro	15 mL
½ tsp	chili powder	2 mL
¼ cup	plain yogurt	60 mL
2 tbsp	freshly squeezed lime juice	30 mL
2 tsp	red wine vinegar	10 mL
2 tsp	liquid honey	10 mL
¼ cup	extra virgin olive oil	60 mL
	Kosher salt	
	Freshly ground black pepper	

1. Using a spiralizer, cut zucchini and carrots into medium strands. Trim strands to desired length.

2. In a medium serving bowl, combine zucchini, carrots, tomatoes and beans.

3. In a small bowl, whisk together garlic, cilantro, chili powder, yogurt, lime juice, vinegar and honey. Gradually whisk in oil.

4. Pour dressing over salad and toss to combine.

Mandarin-Style Tofu Salad

If you are looking for a recipe that is short on time but long on flavor and packs a powerful punch, you will enjoy this entrée-worthy salad.

Tips

To drain the tofu, cut it into 1-inch (2.5 cm) slabs, then place it between several sheets of paper towel. Press with the bottom of the cast-iron skillet to release the majority of the moisture.

When spiralizing, you always end up with a little bit of vegetable or fruit that is too small to spiralize. I use these pieces to taste-test my dressing before adding it to the salad.

▶ **Large cast-iron skillet**

6 tbsp	minced garlic	90 mL
1 tsp	kosher salt	5 mL
¼ cup	grapeseed oil	60 mL
2 tbsp	sesame oil	30 mL
2 tbsp	rice vinegar	30 mL
3 tbsp	liquid honey	45 mL
1½ tbsp	olive oil	22 mL
12 oz	firm tofu, drained, patted dry and cut into 1-inch (2.5 cm) cubes	375 g
2	cucumbers, ends cut flat	2
2	carrots, peeled and ends cut flat	2
1	daikon radish, peeled and ends cut flat	1
½ cup	chopped fresh cilantro	125 mL

1. In a small bowl, combine garlic, salt, grapeseed oil, sesame oil, vinegar and honey. Set aside.

2. In cast-iron skillet, heat olive oil over medium heat. Add tofu and cook, stirring, for 10 minutes or until browned and crispy on all sides.

3. Meanwhile, using a spiralizer, cut cucumbers into wide ribbons and pat dry. Cut carrots and radish into thin strands. Trim all ribbons and strands to 4-inch (10 cm) lengths.

4. In a large bowl, combine tofu, spiralized vegetables and cilantro. Add dressing and toss to combine.

Hot-and-Sour Mushroom, Cabbage and Squash Noodle Soup

Deceptively simple, this soup has a complex combination of spicy and tangy flavors, earthy textured mushrooms and silken cabbage. What more could you ask for on a cold winter evening?

Tips

This soup can be served as a starter for up to 8 people. It would go extremely well with Mandarin-Style Tofu Salad (page 143).

Instead of cremini mushrooms, you can use portobello or porcini mushrooms. I would not recommend the small white button mushrooms, as they do not have as much flavor and their texture is less firm.

1	butternut squash neck (at least 4 inches/10 cm long)	1
¼	head green cabbage, outer leaves removed and ends cut flat	¼
2 tsp	virgin coconut oil	10 mL
2 oz	cremini mushrooms, thinly sliced	60 g
3	cloves garlic, minced	3
1 tsp	minced gingerroot	5 mL
1 tbsp	hot pepper flakes	15 mL
2 tbsp	freshly squeezed lime juice	30 mL
4 cups	ready-to-use reduced-sodium vegetable broth	1 L
1 tbsp	soy sauce	15 mL
	Additional soy sauce (optional)	
	Hot pepper sauce, such as Sriracha (optional)	

1. Peel squash neck and trim to 4 inches (10 cm) long, with flat ends. Using a spiralizer, cut squash into wide ribbons. Cut cabbage into medium strands, keeping them separate.

2. In a Dutch oven, heat coconut oil over medium-high heat. Add mushrooms and cook, stirring, for 6 to 8 minutes or until mushrooms have released their liquid and are starting to brown. Add garlic, ginger, hot pepper flakes and lime juice; cook, stirring, for about 1 minute or until fragrant.

3. Stir in broth, reduce heat to medium and bring to a simmer. Add squash and cook, stirring for 3 minutes. Add cabbage and soy sauce; cook, stirring, for 5 to 7 minutes or until cooked to desired tenderness. Serve immediately with soy sauce and hot pepper sauce, if desired.

Grilled Scallop Tacos and Cabbage Slaw with Spicy Avocado Sauce (page 98)

Hungarian Pork Stew with Kohlrabi Noodles (page 132)

Twisted Thai Salad with Peanut Lime Dressing (page 135)

Easy Lentil Marinara with Zucchini Spaghetti (page 164)

Sweet Potato Pizza (page 174)

Kaleidoscope Salad (page 202)

Parsnip Spaghetti with Pine Nut Basil Pesto (page 211)

Spiralized Fruit Tarts (page 217)

Squash Noodles with Sautéed Spinach and Mushrooms

The soft, creamy goodness of delicate summer squash is topped with a delectable combination of spinach, mushrooms and garlic.

Tip

Leeks are grown packed in sandy soil and retain this soil right into your kitchen. To clean them, cut the root ends and green tops off. Trim to 4-inch (10 cm) sections, then slice down the full length of the leek. Separate the sections and add to a large bowl filled with cold water. Using your fingers, rinse off any remaining dirt. The leeks will float and the dirt will fall to the bottom. Pat dry before slicing.

2	yellow summer squash, ends cut flat	2
1 tbsp	olive oil	15 mL
1	small leek (white parts only), thinly sliced	1
6 oz	mushrooms, sliced	175 g
2	cloves garlic, minced	2
½ cup	ready-to-use vegetable broth	125 mL
2 cups	baby spinach	500 mL
2 tbsp	dry white wine (optional)	30 mL
	Kosher salt (optional)	
	Freshly ground black pepper (optional)	

1. Using a spiralizer, cut squash into thin strands. Set aside.

2. In a large skillet, heat oil over medium heat. Add leek and cook, stirring, until just softened. Add mushrooms and cook, stirring, for 3 to 5 minutes or until softened and lightly browned. Add garlic and cook, stirring, for 30 seconds.

3. Stir in squash and broth; cook, stirring, for 2 minutes. Add spinach and cook, stirring, for 30 seconds or until squash is cooked to desired tenderness and spinach is wilted. Stir in wine (if using). If desired, season to taste with salt and pepper.

Squash Ribbons with Baby Artichokes and Asparagus

Baby artichokes and delicate asparagus are punctuated by sweet ribbons of butternut squash in this dish that will generate oohs and aahs from the most discriminating of palates.

**MAKES
6 SERVINGS**

Tip

To choose the best baby artichokes, pick them up and give them a squeeze. Those that are at ideal ripeness will give off a tiny squeak. Do not be tempted to buy the big artichokes. While their flavor may be similar, the outer leaves of baby artichokes are much more tender, and there is less bristly texture near the heart — which is the most flavorful and tender part.

1	butternut squash neck (at least 4 inches/10 cm long)	1
2¾ cups	cold water, divided	675 mL
	Grated zest and juice of 1 lemon	
24	baby artichokes, stem cut to base and 1 inch (2.5 cm) of top trimmed	24
4 tbsp	olive oil (approx.), divided	60 mL
1 lb	asparagus, trimmed and cut diagonally into 2-inch (5 cm) pieces	500 g
1 tbsp	chopped fresh parsley	15 mL
1 tsp	chopped fresh thyme	5 mL
½ tsp	kosher salt	2 mL
¼ tsp	freshly ground black pepper	1 mL
2 tbsp	sesame oil	30 mL
1 cup	freshly grated Parmigiano-Reggiano cheese	250 mL

1. Peel squash neck and trim to 4 inches (10 cm) long, with flat ends. Using a spiralizer, cut squash into wide ribbons. Set aside.

2. In a large bowl, combine 2 cups (500 mL) cold water and lemon juice. Remove dark green outer leaves from artichokes and cut in half, top to bottom. Add artichokes to lemon water as you prepare each one.

3. Working in batches, remove artichokes from lemon water and pat dry. In a large skillet, heat 1 tbsp (15 mL) olive oil over medium heat. Add artichokes, cover and cook, stirring occasionally, for 8 minutes. Uncover and increase heat to medium-high; cook, stirring, for 2 minutes or until artichokes are golden. Using a slotted spoon, transfer artichokes to a large bowl. Repeat until all artichokes are cooked, adding more oil as needed between batches.

I love topping this dish with authentic, full-flavored Parmigiano-Reggiano because it adds intense, complex flavors to the decadent vegetables. You can substitute Parmesan cheese, if desired.

4. Add the remaining cold water to the skillet and bring to a simmer over medium-high heat. Reduce heat to medium, add asparagus, cover and cook, stirring occasionally, for 5 minutes or until tender-crisp. Using a slotted spoon, transfer asparagus to the bowl with the artichokes.

5. Drain any remaining liquid from the skillet and wipe dry. Add 2 tbsp (30 mL) olive oil and heat over medium heat. Add squash ribbons and cook, stirring, for 6 to 8 minutes or until cooked to desired tenderness. Using tongs, transfer to the bowl with the artichoke mixture.

6. To the artichoke mixture, add lemon zest, parsley, thyme, salt, pepper and sesame oil, tossing to combine. Transfer to individual serving bowls and garnish with cheese.

Roasted Butternut Squash and Asparagus with Variegated Pasta

Roasting highlights the sweetness and tenderness of the butternut squash and asparagus. Enticing strands of butternut squash and zucchini round out this colorful, delectable dish.

**MAKES
6 SERVINGS**

Tip

When peeling butternut squash, make sure to remove not only the outer skin, but also the next layer of lighter flesh just inside the skin. You want to use only the orange-yellow flesh.

▸ **Preheat oven to 400°F (200°C), with one rack in the upper third and one in the bottom third**
▸ **2 rimmed baking sheets, lined with foil**

2	butternut squash with necks at least 4 inches (10 cm) long	2
2	small zucchini, ends cut flat	2
5 tbsp	olive oil, divided	75 mL
	Kosher salt	
1 lb	asparagus, trimmed and cut into 2-inch (5 cm) lengths	500 g
½ cup	shredded Monterey Jack cheese	125 mL
⅓ cup	dry white wine	75 mL

1. Cut squash bulbs from necks. Peel butternut squash necks and trim to 4 inches (10 cm) long, with flat ends. Using a spiralizer, cut squash necks and zucchini into medium strands, keeping them separate. Set aside.

2. Peel butternut squash bulbs, cut in half and remove seeds. Cut into 1-inch (2.5 cm) cubes. Place on a prepared baking sheet, drizzle with 2 tbsp (30 mL) oil and toss to coat. Spread out in a single layer and season liberally with salt.

3. Place asparagus on the other prepared baking sheet. Drizzle with 2 tbsp (30 mL) oil and toss to coat. Spread out in a single layer and season liberally with salt.

Tips

Choose zucchini that are straight and fairly even in diameter. This will make it easier to spiral-cut them evenly.

4. Place one baking sheet in the upper third of the preheated oven and the other in the bottom third. Bake for 10 minutes. Pull out baking sheets and turn vegetables. Return to the oven, swapping the sheets' positions on the racks. Bake for 10 to 15 minutes or until vegetables are browned and just tender.

5. Meanwhile, in a large skillet, heat the remaining oil over medium heat. Add squash strands and cook, stirring, for 4 to 6 minutes or until starting to soften. Add zucchini strands, cheese and wine; cook, tossing, for 2 to 3 minutes or until cheese is melted and vegetables are cooked to desired consistency.

6. Transfer squash mixture to a serving plate or bowls. Top with roasted asparagus and squash cubes. Serve immediately.

Lazy Sunday Fettuccine with Peas and Sage Sauce

Vegetarians and vegans will find comfort in this creamy baked casserole with a savory, cheesy blend of sage, peas and zucchini.

MAKES 4 SERVINGS

Tip

Vegan Parmesan: In a food processor, process 1 cup (250 mL) whole raw almonds, ¼ cup (60 mL) nutritional yeast and ½ tsp (2 mL) kosher salt until fluffy and no chunks of nuts remain. This recipe is easily doubled and can be stored in an airtight container in the refrigerator for up to 1 month.

▶ **Preheat oven to 375°F (190°C)**

▶ **8-cup (2 L) shallow casserole dish**

5	zucchini, ends cut flat	5
1 cup	frozen peas	250 mL
¼ cup	water	60 mL
¼ cup	butter or vegan buttery spread	60 mL
12	fresh sage leaves, chopped	12
¾ cup	freshly grated Parmesan cheese or Vegan Parmesan (see tip, at left)	175 mL
Pinch	kosher salt	Pinch
Pinch	freshly ground black pepper	Pinch
	Additional freshly grated Parmesan cheese or Vegan Parmesan (optional)	

1. Using a spiralizer, cut zucchini into medium strands. Set aside.

2. In a medium saucepan, combine peas and water. Bring to a simmer over medium heat. Cover and cook, stirring occasionally, for 5 minutes or until peas are tender and water is absorbed.

3. In a large skillet, melt butter over medium heat. Add sage and cook, stirring, for 1 to 2 minutes or until slightly crispy. Add zucchini and cook, stirring, for 1 to 2 minutes or until just tender. Add peas, Parmesan, salt and pepper; toss to coat. Transfer to casserole dish.

4. Bake in preheated oven for 5 to 10 minutes or until lightly browned. Garnish with additional Parmesan, if desired.

Down-Home Noodles
with Tomatoes and Pesto

A classic basil pesto adds robust flavor to this colorful company-worthy dish.

Tips

To make this dish vegan, substitute nutritional yeast or Vegan Parmesan (see tip, page 150) for the traditional Parmesan.

Cherry tomatoes come in a variety of colors and flavors. Using several different colors will up the wow factor of this dish.

▶ **Food processor**

1	clove garlic, coarsely chopped	1
1 cup	packed fresh basil	250 mL
¼ cup	freshly grated Parmesan cheese (see tip, at left)	60 mL
	Kosher salt	
	Freshly ground black pepper	
3 tbsp	extra virgin olive oil	45 mL
3	zucchini, ends cut flat	3
1 cup	cherry tomatoes, halved	250 mL
	Additional freshly grated Parmesan cheese (optional)	

1. In food processor, combine garlic, basil, cheese, salt and pepper; process until smooth. With the motor running, through the feed tube, gradually add oil. Set aside.

2. Using a spiralizer, cut zucchini into thin strands.

3. In a serving bowl, combine zucchini, tomatoes and pesto, tossing to coat. Garnish with additional cheese, if desired.

Hearty Mushroom Marinara over Sweet Potato Noodles

Even the pickiest of eaters will enjoy this richly flavored, hearty sauce that highlights the flavor of the sweet potato noodles. The mushrooms add a meaty texture and earthy flavor to complete the experience.

MAKES 4 TO 6 SERVINGS

Tip

If you want to use fresh tomatoes instead of canned, you will need about 3 lbs (1.5 kg). Blanch tomatoes in boiling water for 30 to 60 seconds, then plunge them into ice-cold water. Remove skins and core. Cut tomatoes into quarters. Add to a saucepan over medium-high heat and bring to a boil, crushing tomatoes with a potato masher. Boil gently until tomatoes are softened and evenly crushed. Add to the recipe in step 3.

4	sweet potatoes, peeled and ends cut flat	4
2	carrots, peeled and ends cut flat	2
1	onion, peeled and ends cut flat	1
6 tbsp	olive oil, divided	90 mL
1	stalk celery, chopped	1
2	cloves garlic, minced	2
1 lb	button mushrooms, finely chopped	500 g
12 oz	shiitake mushrooms, stems discarded, caps finely chopped	375 g
¼ cup	tomato paste	60 mL
1	can (28 oz/796 mL) crushed tomatoes	1
8	fresh basil leaves, chopped	8
¼ cup	packed fresh parsley, chopped	60 mL
1 tbsp	dried oregano	15 mL
	Garlic powder	
	Kosher salt	
	Freshly ground black pepper	
¼ cup	freshly grated Parmesan cheese (optional)	60 mL

1. Using a spiralizer, cut sweet potatoes, carrots and onion into thin strands, keeping them separate. Trim carrot and onion strands to 3-inch (7.5 cm) lengths.

2. In a large skillet, heat 2 tbsp (30 mL) oil over medium heat. Add carrots, onion and celery; cook, stirring, for 7 to 9 minutes or until softened and onion is translucent. Add garlic and cook, stirring, for 1 to 2 minutes or until softened. Transfer mixture to a large saucepan.

Garlic powder is used to season the sweet potato strands because it adheres evenly to the strands along with the salt and pepper. You could instead use garlic salt and eliminate the kosher salt. If you prefer to use fresh garlic, mince 2 cloves and sprinkle them over the strands.

3. Add 2 tbsp (30 mL) oil to the skillet and increase heat to medium-high. Add button and shiitake mushrooms and cook, stirring occasionally, for 15 to 20 minutes or until mushrooms have released their liquid and are lightly browned. Stir in tomato paste. Add tomatoes, scraping up any brown bits from the bottom of the pan. Transfer mixture to the large saucepan.

4. Place the saucepan over medium-low heat. Stir in basil, parsley and oregano; simmer, stirring occasionally, for 25 to 30 minutes or until thickened.

5. Meanwhile, in the large skillet, heat the remaining oil over medium heat. Add sweet potato strands and season to taste with garlic powder, salt and pepper. Cook, stirring, for 6 to 8 minutes or until cooked to desired tenderness.

6. Transfer sweet potatoes to sauce and toss to combine. Serve garnished with Parmesan, if desired.

Squash Pasta with Rich and Hearty Mushroom Bolognese

Your whole family will want to dive right in to this aromatic, robust sauce that will satisfy even the heartiest of appetites.

**MAKES
6 SERVINGS**

Tip

After spiralizing bell peppers, you will need to remove the white flesh and seeds from the strands. Alternatively, you can core the peppers, but they will not hold their shape as well during spiralizing.

2	carrots, peeled and ends cut flat	2
1	onion, peeled and ends cut flat	1
1	green bell pepper, stem removed (see tip, at left)	1
½ cup	olive oil, divided	125 mL
2	stalks celery, diced	2
5	cloves garlic, minced	5
¼ cup	chopped fresh sage	60 mL
¼ cup	chopped fresh basil	60 mL
2	bay leaves	2
2 cups	ready-to-use reduced-sodium vegetable broth	500 mL
2 tbsp	red wine vinegar	30 mL
1 lb	button mushrooms, diced	500 g
12 oz	shiitake mushrooms, stems discarded (see tip, opposite), caps finely diced	375 g
¼ cup	tomato paste	60 mL
1	can (28 oz/796 mL) crushed tomatoes	1
¾ cup	unsweetened almond milk	175 mL
2 tbsp	tamari	30 mL
	Kosher salt	
	Freshly ground black pepper	
6	yellow summer squash, ends cut flat	6
3 tbsp	chopped fresh parsley	45 mL

1. Using a spiralizer, cut carrots into medium strands and trim to 3-inch (7.5) lengths. Cut onion into medium strands and chop. Cut green pepper into wide ribbons, remove white flesh and seeds, and chop ribbons.

Tip

Shiitake mushroom stems are very tough and can be difficult to remove. To make sure you remove all of the stem, grip it firmly near the base and twist. Try not to remove any of the meaty flesh from the underside of the cap.

2. In a large skillet, heat 3 tbsp (45 mL) oil over medium heat. Add carrots, onion, green pepper and celery; cook, stirring occasionally, for 7 to 10 minutes or until softened. Add garlic, sage and basil; cook, stirring, for 1 minute or until aromatic. Add bay leaves, broth and vinegar; increase heat to medium-high and boil, stirring, for 5 to 7 minutes or until liquid is almost evaporated. Transfer mixture to a large saucepan.

3. Add the remaining oil to the skillet and heat over medium-high heat. Add button and shiitake mushrooms and cook, stirring occasionally, for 15 to 20 minutes or until mushrooms have released their liquid and are lightly browned. Stir in tomato paste. Add tomatoes, scraping up any brown bits from the bottom of the pan. Transfer mixture to the large saucepan.

4. Place the saucepan over medium-low heat and stir in almond milk and tamari. Simmer, stirring occasionally, for 30 to 45 minutes or until thickened. Season to taste with salt and pepper.

5. Meanwhile, using a spiralizer, cut squash into medium strands.

6. Add squash and parsley to sauce. Increase heat to medium and cook, stirring, for 2 to 3 minutes or until squash is cooked to desired tenderness. Serve immediately.

Caprese Beet Noodle Pasta

Roasted beets and tomatoes combine with mozzarella in a warm and inviting dish that makes a great starter or light lunch.

MAKES 4 TO 6 SERVINGS

Tips

To make halving the tomatoes a breeze, lay them on a small plate. Turn another same-size plate upside down on top. Use a sharp knife to cut the tomatoes horizontally between the plates.

Mini balls of mozzarella cheese are frequently called bocconcini. They range from the size of a cherry tomato to the size of an egg. The cherry tomato size is ideal for this recipe.

▷ **Preheat oven to 400°F (200°C)**
▷ **Rimmed baking sheet, lined with foil**

4	beets, ends cut flat	4
10	cherry tomatoes, halved	10
	Olive oil	
	Kosher salt	
	Freshly ground black pepper	
2	cloves garlic, minced	2
4	mini balls fresh mozzarella cheese (see tip, at left)	4
2 tbsp	chopped fresh parsley	30 mL

1. Using a spiralizer, cut beets into wide ribbons. Set aside.

2. Place tomatoes, skin side down, at one end of the prepared baking sheet. Drizzle with oil and season with salt and pepper. Roast in preheated oven for 5 minutes.

3. Add beets to the other end of the baking sheet, spreading them out loosely. Drizzle with olive oil and season with salt. Sprinkle garlic over tomatoes and beets. Roast for 5 to 7 minutes, tossing beets once, until beets have softened and slightly darkened. Drop mozzarella balls on top of beets. Bake for 2 minutes or until mozzarella is softened.

4. Divide beets evenly among serving plates and top with roasted tomatoes. Garnish with parsley.

Squash Spaghetti with Butter-Roasted Tomato Sauce

You may never eat another sauce after trying this simple, deeply flavored roasted tomato sauce with a surprise ingredient (dulse flakes) that adds some umami.

**MAKES
4 SERVINGS**

Tips

Dulse is a sea vegetable harvested in the cold waters of the North Atlantic and then dried. Dulse flakes add a tangy, slightly salty flavor to this dish.

I recommend using unsalted butter in this recipe because the dulse flakes and canned tomatoes both add salt. If you choose to use salted butter, use a reduced-sodium vegetable broth and/ or reduced-salt canned crushed tomatoes.

The tomato sauce can be prepared ahead as in step 2. Let cool, cover and refrigerate for up to 4 days. When ready to cook, proceed with step 3.

▸ **Preheat oven to 425°F (220°C)**
▸ **13- by 9-inch (33 by 23 cm) glass baking dish**

1	butternut squash neck (at least 4 inches/10 cm long)	1
8	cloves garlic, minced	8
1	can (28 oz/796 mL) crushed tomatoes	1
2 tbsp	dulse flakes	30 mL
1/2 tsp	hot pepper flakes	2 mL
Pinch	freshly ground black pepper (optional)	Pinch
1/4 cup	unsalted butter, cut into small pieces	60 mL
1/2 cup	ready-to-use vegetable broth	125 mL
	Freshly grated Parmesan cheese (optional)	

1. Peel butternut squash neck and trim to 4 inches (10 cm) long, with flat ends. Using a spiralizer, cut squash into wide ribbons. Set aside.

2. In prepared baking dish, combine garlic, tomatoes, dulse flakes, hot pepper flakes, black pepper (if using) and butter. Bake in preheated oven for 35 to 40 minutes, stirring occasionally, until thick and sticky. Transfer mixture to a large saucepan.

3. Add broth to tomato sauce in saucepan and bring to a boil over medium-high heat. Add squash, reduce heat to medium and simmer, stirring, for 2 to 3 minutes or until squash is cooked to desired tenderness. Serve garnished with cheese, if desired.

Zucchini Fettuccine with Creamy Butternut Rosemary Sauce

If you love creamy sauces that are bursting with flavor, you will want to dive right in to this partnership of creamy butternut squash, garlic and rosemary flowing over mushrooms and zucchini.

MAKES
4 SERVINGS

Tip

Before slicing the mushrooms, trim the bottom of the stems. If the gills on the underside of the caps have not opened, you can slice the mushrooms as is. If they have opened, you may want to remove the stems and scrape out the gills before slicing the caps and stems. The gills won't affect the taste, but they will change the color of the sauce to a darker brown.

▸ **Preheat oven to 375°F (190°C)**
▸ **Rimmed baking sheet, lined with foil**
▸ **Blender**

5	zucchini, ends cut flat	5
1	onion, peeled and ends cut flat	1
1	butternut squash neck (at least 4 inches/10 cm long)	1
3 tbsp	olive oil, divided	45 mL
2	cloves garlic, minced	2
2 tsp	fresh minced rosemary	10 mL
1 cup	coconut milk, heavy cream or whipping (35%) cream	250 mL
½ cup	ready-to-use vegetable broth	125 mL
8 oz	cremini mushrooms, sliced (see tip, at left)	250 g
	Freshly ground black pepper (optional)	

1. Cut zucchini and onion into medium strands, keeping them separate. Set aside.

2. Peel butternut squash neck and trim to 4 inches (10 cm) long, with flat ends. Using a spiralizer, cut squash into wide ribbons.

3. Place squash ribbons on prepared baking sheet, drizzle with 1 tbsp (15 mL) oil and toss to combine. Separate ribbons on pan so they are not touching. Bake in preheated oven for 8 to 10 minutes, tossing halfway through, until squash is softened. Let cool. Transfer to blender.

Tip

The bulbous end of the butternut squash contains seeds, so it does not spiralize well. Try roasting it instead, for a luscious side dish with any meal. Peel the squash, remove seeds and cut into 1½-inch (4 cm) cubes. Toss with melted butter, brown sugar, salt and pepper and roast in a 400°F (200°C) oven for 20 to 25 minutes.

4. In a large skillet, heat 1 tbsp (15 mL) oil over medium heat. Add onion strands and cook, stirring, for 3 to 5 minutes or until translucent. Add garlic and cook, stirring, for 30 seconds. Transfer to blender.

5. Add rosemary, coconut milk and broth to blender and blend until smooth. Set aside.

6. In the skillet, heat the remaining oil over medium heat. Add mushrooms and cook, stirring, for 5 to 7 minutes or until they have released their liquid and are starting to brown. Add the blended sauce and cook, stirring, for 3 to 4 minutes or until warmed through. Add zucchini strands and cook, stirring, for 2 to 3 minutes or until cooked to desired tenderness. Serve sprinkled with pepper, if using.

Creamy Vegan Red Pepper Alfredo over Zucchini Noodles

For a full-flavored, creamy, decadent sauce that brings zucchini noodles to a new level, dive into this incredibly satisfying pasta dish that will impress even the most discriminating of foodies.

Tips

After spiralizing bell peppers, you will need to remove the white flesh and seeds from the strands. Alternatively, you can core the peppers, but they will not hold their shape as well during spiralizing.

Choose zucchini that are straight and fairly even in diameter. This will make it easier to spiral-cut them evenly.

▸ **Rimmed baking sheet, lined with foil**
▸ **Blender or food processor**

1 cup	raw cashews	250 mL
2 cups	water	500 mL
2	tomatoes, cut in half	2
2 tbsp	olive oil, divided	30 mL
	Kosher salt	
	Freshly ground black pepper	
2	red bell peppers, stems removed (see tip, at left)	2
1 cup	ready-to-use reduced-sodium vegetable broth	250 mL
1	clove garlic, minced	1
1 tbsp	chopped fresh basil	15 mL
1 tsp	dried oregano	5 mL
1 tsp	balsamic vinegar	5 mL
4	zucchini, ends cut flat	4

1. Place cashews in a medium bowl and cover with water. Let soak for 30 minutes or until fully softened.

2. Meanwhile, preheat oven to 450°F (230°C).

3. Place tomatoes, skin side down, at one end of the prepared baking sheet. Drizzle with 1 tbsp (15 mL) olive oil and season with salt and pepper.

The roasted tomatoes and peppers can be prepared ahead of time. Refrigerate separately in airtight containers for up to 1 week or freeze for up to 2 months.

4. Using a spiralizer, cut red peppers into wide ribbons and remove white flesh and seeds. Add to the other end of the baking sheet. Drizzle with the remaining olive oil and season with salt.

5. Bake in preheated oven for 12 to 15 minutes or until tomatoes and peppers are wrinkled and lightly charred. Remove from oven and cover tightly with foil. Let stand for 10 to 15 minutes. Remove skin from peppers.

6. Drain cashews and discard water. Rinse cashews until water runs clear. In blender, combine roasted tomatoes and peppers, cashews and broth; blend until smooth. Transfer to a large skillet.

7. Add garlic, basil, oregano and vinegar to the skillet and cook over medium-low heat, stirring, for 7 to 9 minutes or until heated through.

8. Meanwhile, using a spiralizer, cut zucchini into medium strands.

9. Add zucchini to skillet and cook, stirring, for 2 to 3 minutes or until cooked to desired tenderness.

Vegan Roasted Red Pepper Cream Sauce with Zucchini Noodles

This velvety, peppery cream sauce adds a rich yet light blanket to fresh zucchini noodles, for a tour de force of flavor.

MAKES 4 SERVINGS

Tip

Vegan Parmesan: In a food processor, process 1 cup (250 mL) whole raw almonds, ¼ cup (60 mL) nutritional yeast and ½ tsp (2 mL) kosher salt until fluffy and no chunks of nuts remain. This recipe is easily doubled and can be stored in an airtight container in the refrigerator for up to 1 month.

▶ **Preheat oven to 450°F (230°C)**
▶ **Rimmed baking sheet, lined with foil**
▶ **Blender or food processor**

3	red bell peppers	3
4	zucchini, ends cut flat	4
2 tbsp	olive oil	30 mL
2	shallots, finely chopped	2
4	cloves garlic, minced	4
Pinch	kosher salt	Pinch
Pinch	freshly ground black pepper	Pinch
2 tbsp	nutritional yeast	30 mL
1½ tbsp	cornstarch	22 mL
Pinch	hot pepper flakes	Pinch
1½ cups	unsweetened almond milk	375 mL
	Vegan Parmesan (see tip, at left)	
	Finely chopped fresh parsley (optional)	

1. Place peppers on prepared baking sheet. Roast in preheated oven for 25 to 30 minutes, turning occasionally, until wrinkled and lightly charred. Remove from oven, cover tightly with foil and let stand for 10 to 15 minutes. Remove and discard skin, seeds and stems. Set aside.

2. Meanwhile, using a spiralizer, cut zucchini into medium strands. Set aside.

Tip

Roasted peppers can be made ahead of time. Refrigerate in an airtight container, with any leftover juices, for up to 1 week. You can also cover them in olive oil and refrigerate for up to 3 weeks. You might like to make a larger batch for use in other recipes or as a snack.

3. In a large skillet, heat oil over medium heat. Add shallots and cook, stirring, for 1 to 2 minutes or until softened and lightly browned. Add garlic and cook, stirring, for 30 seconds. Season with salt and black pepper.

4. In blender, combine shallot mixture, roasted peppers, nutritional yeast, cornstarch, hot pepper flakes and almond milk; blend until smooth.

5. Transfer sauce to skillet and bring to a simmer over medium heat, stirring. Reduce heat to low and cook, stirring, for 4 to 6 minutes or until thickened. Add zucchini and cook, stirring, for 2 to 3 minutes or until cooked to desired tenderness. Serve garnished with Parmesan and parsley (if using).

Easy Lentil Marinara with Zucchini Spaghetti

This deeply flavored and hearty lentil marinara is served over light zucchini noodles. Best of all, you can make the sauce ahead of time and then just reheat it, spiralize your noodles and serve on a busy weeknight.

MAKES 4 SERVINGS

Tip

For best results, use French green (Puy) lentils. They will stay firmer when cooked and have a nuttier flavor, which adds interest and depth to the marinara sauce.

1 cup	dried French green lentils (Puy lentils), rinsed	250 mL
3 cups	water	750 mL
2 tbsp	olive oil, divided	30 mL
1	onion, chopped	1
2	cloves garlic, minced	2
2	cans (each 14 oz/398 mL) diced tomatoes, with juice	2
2 tbsp	minced reconstituted sun-dried tomatoes	30 mL
1 tsp	dried basil	5 mL
1 tsp	dried oregano	5 mL
½ tsp	dried thyme	2 mL
	Kosher salt (optional)	
	Freshly ground black pepper (optional)	
6	zucchini, ends cut flat	6
	Freshly grated Parmesan cheese (optional)	

1. In a medium saucepan, bring lentils and water to a boil over high heat. Reduce heat to low, cover and simmer, stirring occasionally, for 45 to 60 minutes or until lentils are tender. Drain.

2. In a large skillet, heat 1 tbsp (15 mL) oil over medium heat. Add onion and cook, stirring, for 5 to 7 minutes or until translucent. Add garlic and cook, stirring, for 1 minute.

The lentil marinara can be made ahead and stored in an airtight container in the refrigerator for up to 3 days or in the freezer for up to 3 months. Reheat before using. Spiralize the zucchini and cook it just before serving.

3. Reduce heat to medium-low and stir in diced tomatoes, sun-dried tomatoes, basil, oregano and thyme. If desired, season to taste with salt and pepper. Cook, stirring occasionally, for 10 to 15 minutes or until slightly thickened. Add lentils and cook, stirring, for 5 minutes.

4. Meanwhile, using a spiralizer, cut zucchini into thin strands.

5. In another large skillet, heat the remaining oil over medium heat. Add zucchini and cook, stirring, for 2 to 3 minutes or until cooked to desired tenderness.

6. Divide zucchini among four plates and top with sauce. Garnish with Parmesan (if using).

Springy Spiralized Spaghetti alla Carbonara

This classic spaghetti dish is always a favorite. Change it up with zucchini noodles instead of wheat pasta, and don't be surprised if you have just added a new favorite to your family meals.

MAKES 2 SERVINGS

Tips

When you add the egg mixture to the hot skillet, stir quickly to coat the zucchini. You want to be sure that the strands are coated before the eggs have a chance to cook.

To make this dish vegan, substitute nutritional yeast or Vegan Parmesan (see tip, page 162) for the Parmesan cheese.

3	zucchini, ends cut flat	3
4	medium or large eggs, at room temperature	4
¼ cup	coconut milk	60 mL
Pinch	freshly ground black pepper	Pinch
1 tbsp	virgin coconut oil	15 mL
2	cloves garlic, minced	2
	Freshly grated Parmesan cheese (optional)	
	Coarsely chopped fresh parsley (optional)	

1. Using a spiralizer, cut zucchini into thin strands. Set aside.

2. In a medium bowl, whisk together eggs, coconut milk and pepper.

3. In a large skillet, heat coconut oil over medium heat. Add garlic and cook, stirring, for 30 seconds or until fragrant. Add zucchini and cook, stirring, for 2 to 3 minutes or until cooked to desired tenderness.

4. Remove skillet from heat and add egg mixture, stirring to coat noodles. Continue stirring until eggs are cooked and slightly thickened. If desired, serve garnished with Parmesan and parsley.

Spicy Tofu with Spiral Zucchini, Red Pepper and Lime

Kick your spiral zucchini strands up a notch with a spicy seasoning contrasted with cool lime and coconut for an interesting and truly satisfying flavor.

Tips

Dulse is a sea vegetable harvested in the cold waters of the North Atlantic and then dried. Dulse flakes add a tangy, slightly salty flavor to this dish.

For an elegant garnish, instead of roughly chopping the basil, you can cut it into chiffonade. Remove stems and stack 10 or more leaves together. Roll the leaves lengthwise into a fairly tight spiral, then cut crosswise into thin strips. Fluff the strips.

▶ Mortar and pestle

4	zucchini, ends cut flat	4
1	red bell pepper, stem removed	1
3	cloves garlic, coarsely chopped	3
2	shallots, coarsely chopped	2
1 tbsp	¼-inch (0.5 cm) gingerroot pieces	15 mL
2 tbsp	peanut oil, divided	30 mL
12 oz	extra-firm tofu, drained, patted dry and cut into ½-inch (1 cm) cubes	375 g
1 tsp	dulse flakes	5 mL
Pinch	cayenne pepper	Pinch
1⅓ cups	coconut milk	325 mL
3 tbsp	freshly squeezed lime juice	45 mL
1½ tbsp	tamari	22 mL
3 tbsp	fresh basil, roughly chopped	45 mL

1. Using a spiralizer, cut zucchini into thin strands. Cut red pepper into wide ribbons, keeping them separate, remove white flesh and seeds, and chop ribbons. Set aside.

2. Using a mortar and pestle, grind garlic, shallots and ginger into a fine paste. Set aside.

3. In a large skillet, heat 1 tbsp (15 mL) oil over medium heat. Add tofu and cook, stirring, for 5 to 6 minutes or until golden brown on all sides. Transfer tofu to a bowl.

4. Add the remaining oil to the skillet and heat over medium-high heat. Add red pepper and cook, stirring, for 3 to 4 minutes or until softened.

5. Return tofu to the skillet. Add garlic paste and cook, stirring, until fragrant. Add dulse flakes, cayenne, coconut milk, lime juice and tamari; reduce heat to medium-low and cook, stirring, for 3 to 4 minutes or until sauce is slightly thickened. Add zucchini and cook, stirring, for 2 to 3 minutes or until cooked to desired tenderness. Serve garnished with basil.

Bountiful Thai Tofu with Peanut Sauce

The exhilarating flavors of this peanut sauce tossed with a variety of sensations, from crispy tofu and stir-fried veggies to crunchy peanuts, make for a delicious, substantial meal.

MAKES 4 TO 6 SERVINGS

Tips

To drain the tofu, cut it into 1-inch (2.5 cm) slabs, then place it between several sheets of paper towel. Press with the bottom of the skillet to release the majority of the moisture. If you do this before starting steps 1 and 2, the tofu will have longer to dry.

After spiralizing bell peppers, you will need to remove the white flesh and seeds from the strands. Alternatively, you can core the peppers, but they will not hold their shape as well during spiralizing.

> ▸ **Preheat oven to 350°F (180°C)**
> ▸ **Mortar and pestle**
> ▸ **Baking sheet, lined with lightly oiled foil**
> ▸ **Steamer basket**

Peanut Sauce

3	cloves garlic, coarsely chopped	3
2	shallots, coarsely chopped	2
1½ tbsp	minced gingerroot, divided	22 mL
1 cup	ready-to-use reduced-sodium vegetable broth	250 mL
½ cup	creamy peanut butter	125 mL
½ cup	coconut milk	125 mL
2 tbsp	tamari	30 mL
1½ tbsp	light (fancy) molasses	22 mL
2 tsp	rice vinegar	10 mL
Dash	hot pepper sauce (such as Sriracha)	Dash

Tofu and Vegetables

1 tbsp	soy sauce	15 mL
1 tbsp	ready-to-use reduced-sodium vegetable broth	15 mL
12 oz	firm tofu, drained, patted dry and cut into 1-inch (2.5 cm) cubes	375 g
3	carrots, peeled and ends cut flat	3
1	head broccoli, florets and stems separated	1
1	red bell pepper, stem removed (see tip, at left)	1
1 tbsp	peanut oil	15 mL
1 tbsp	freshly squeezed lime juice	15 mL
3	green onions, sliced	3
½ cup	roasted peanuts (optional)	125 mL

The peanut sauce can be made ahead and refrigerated in an airtight container for up to 3 days. It makes a great dip for a multitude of vegetables, with snow peas being one of my personal favorites. I like to make extra sauce so I have it on hand for either a light snack or nibbling with some of the broccoli florets while I am making this dish.

1. *Peanut Sauce:* Using a mortar and pestle, grind garlic, shallots and 1 tbsp (15 mL) ginger into a fine paste. Set aside.

2. In a small saucepan, over medium heat, whisk together broth and peanut butter. Add the remaining ginger, garlic paste, coconut milk, tamari, molasses, vinegar and hot pepper sauce. Bring to a simmer and cook, stirring, for 5 minutes. Remove from heat and set aside.

3. *Tofu and Vegetables:* In a small bowl, combine soy sauce and broth. Add tofu and let marinate for at least 30 minutes or up to 4 hours.

4. Transfer tofu to prepared baking sheet. Bake in preheated oven for 20 to 30 minutes, turning once, until browned and crispy but still tender.

5. Meanwhile, using a spiralizer, cut carrots into thin strands. Peel broccoli stems and cut into thin strands. Cut red pepper into wide ribbons, keeping them separate, and remove white flesh and seeds.

6. In a steamer basket set over a saucepan of boiling water, steam broccoli florets for 2 to 4 minutes or until tender-crisp. Using a slotted spoon, transfer florets to a bowl of ice water and let cool for 2 to 3 minutes. Drain and set aside.

7. In a large wok or skillet, heat oil over medium heat. Add red pepper ribbons and cook, stirring, for 2 to 3 minutes or until tender-crisp. Add tofu, carrots and broccoli strands; cook, stirring, for 5 to 7 minutes or until vegetables are cooked to desired tenderness. Stir in broccoli florets during the last minute of cooking to heat through.

8. Meanwhile, return peanut sauce to a simmer over medium heat. Stir in lime juice. Add sauce to wok and stir to combine. Serve garnished with green onions and peanuts (if using).

Kung Pao Tofu and Zoodles

This Chinese-inspired dish takes on a new profile with tofu and zucchini noodles. The flavor combination of salty, sweet, sour and spicy will light up your taste buds.

**MAKES
4 SERVINGS**

Tips

To drain the tofu, cut it into 1-inch (2.5 cm) slabs, then place it between several sheets of paper towel. Press with the bottom of the skillet to release the majority of the moisture. If you do this before starting steps 1 and 2, the tofu will have longer to dry.

After spiralizing bell peppers, you will need to remove the white flesh and seeds from the strands. Alternatively, you can core the peppers, but they will not hold their shape as well during spiralizing.

▶ **Mortar and pestle**

4	zucchini, ends cut flat	4
1	red bell pepper, stem removed (see tip, at left)	1
4	cloves garlic, coarsely chopped	4
2 tsp	¼-inch (0.5 cm) gingerroot pieces	10 mL
2 tbsp	olive oil, divided	30 mL
12 oz	extra-firm tofu, drained, patted dry and cut into ½-inch (1 cm) cubes	375 g
¼ cup	water	60 mL
3 tbsp	tamari or soy sauce	45 mL
2 tbsp	balsamic vinegar	30 mL
2 tsp	sesame oil	10 mL
2 tsp	hoisin sauce	10 mL
2 tsp	pure maple syrup	10 mL
1 tsp	hot pepper sauce (such as Sriracha)	5 mL
¼ cup	crushed unsalted roasted peanuts	60 mL

1. Using a spiralizer, cut zucchini and red pepper into medium strands, keeping them separate. Remove white flesh and seeds from pepper strands. Set aside.

2. Using a mortar and pestle, grind garlic and ginger into a fine paste.

3. In a large skillet, heat 1 tbsp (15 mL) olive oil over medium heat. Add tofu and cook, stirring, for 5 to 6 minutes or until golden brown on all sides. Add garlic paste and cook, stirring, for 30 seconds or until fragrant. Transfer tofu to a plate.

The zucchini will release moisture as it cooks. If you would like to thicken your sauce, add 1 to 2 tsp (5 to 10 mL) coconut flour to the sauce in step 5 and cook, stirring, until thickened to desired consistency.

4. In a small bowl, whisk together water, tamari, vinegar, sesame oil, hoisin sauce, maple syrup and hot pepper sauce. Set aside.

5. Add the remaining olive oil to the skillet and heat over medium heat. Add red pepper strands and tamari mixture; bring to a boil. Reduce heat and simmer, stirring, for 2 to 3 minutes or until sauce is thickened. Add zucchini and cook, stirring, for 2 minutes.

6. Return tofu to the pan and cook, stirring, for 1 minute or until zucchini is cooked to desired tenderness and tofu and zucchini are coated with sauce. Serve immediately, sprinkled with peanuts.

Summer Squash Tart

Colorful zucchini and yellow squash impart a savory flavor to this rustic free-form tart with a beautiful presentation your guests will love.

Tips

Choose zucchini and yellow summer squash that are straight and fairly even in diameter. This will make it easier to spiral-cut them evenly.

You can make your own Italian seasoning blend by combining 1 tsp (5 mL) each dried basil, oregano and thyme.

▶ **Food processor, fitted with dough blade**
▶ **Baking sheet, sprayed with nonstick olive oil cooking spray**

Crust

1½ cups	all-purpose flour	375 mL
¼ tsp	kosher salt	1 mL
½ cup	cold (solid) virgin coconut oil	125 mL
1 tsp	white vinegar	5 mL
6 to 8 tbsp	ice water	90 to 125 mL

Filling

2	zucchini, ends cut flat	2
2	yellow summer squash, ends cut flat	2
1 tbsp	dried Italian seasoning	15 mL
Pinch	kosher salt	Pinch
Pinch	freshly ground black pepper	Pinch
2 tbsp	extra virgin olive oil	30 mL
1	medium or large egg, beaten	1
2 tbsp	water	30 mL

1. *Crust:* In food processor, pulse to combine flour and salt. Add coconut oil and vinegar; pulse until oil is fully incorporated. Through the feed tube, gradually add water as needed, pulsing until mixture starts to form a ball.

2. Flatten dough ball into a disc, wrap with plastic wrap and refrigerate for at least 1 hour or up to 3 hours.

3. *Filling:* Meanwhile, using a spiralizer, cut zucchini and yellow squash into thin strands.

4. In a large bowl, toss zucchini and squash with Italian seasoning, salt, pepper and olive oil. Let stand for 30 minutes to marinate.

Use your favorite marmalade to brush the crust in place of the egg and water mixture.

5. Preheat oven to 375°F (190°C).

6. On a lightly floured surface, roll out dough into a 10½-inch (26.5 cm) circle. Transfer to prepared baking sheet.

7. Using tongs, lift zucchini and squash strands from marinade, shaking off excess marinade. Transfer strands to dough, starting in the center and spiraling outward in concentric circles until you reach 1½ inches (4 cm) from the edge of the crust. Discard marinade.

8. In a small bowl, whisk together egg and water. Brush over exposed crust.

9. Bake for 20 to 25 minutes or until squash is tender and top of crust is crispy. Let cool on a wire rack before cutting and serving.

Sweet Potato Pizza

Inspired by the traditional Southern sweet potato pie, this sweet potato pizza with creamy cheese is a warm and comforting fall treat.

Tip

If you don't want to make the cauliflower crust, you can substitute a store-brought pizza crust.

▷ **Preheat oven to 425°F (220°C)**
▷ **Food processor or blender**
▷ **Colander, lined with cheesecloth, or nut milk bag**
▷ **Baking sheet, lined with parchment paper**

Pizza Crust

1½ lbs	cauliflower florets	750 g
2 tsp	ground flax seeds (flaxseed meal)	10 mL
⅓ cup	crumbled goat cheese	75 mL
1 tsp	minced garlic	5 mL
½ tsp	dried basil	2 mL
½ tsp	dried oregano	2 mL
¼ tsp	kosher salt	1 mL

Toppings

12 oz	cream cheese, softened	375 g
½ tsp	ground nutmeg	2 mL
2	sweet potatoes, peeled and ends cut flat	2
1 tbsp	olive oil	15 mL
½ cup	chopped pecans or walnuts	125 mL
⅓ cup	packed brown sugar	75 mL
2½ tbsp	all-purpose flour	37 mL
1½ tbsp	butter, melted	22 mL

1. *Crust:* In food processor, pulse cauliflower until it resembles damp grains. You should have about 2 cups (500 mL).

2. Transfer cauliflower to a microwave-safe bowl, cover, leaving a small opening to allow steam to escape, and microwave on High for 4 minutes. Carefully pour cauliflower into prepared colander and let drain and cool. Twist the cheesecloth to squeeze out as much liquid as possible, reserving 3 tbsp (45 mL) liquid. Add flax seeds to reserved liquid and mix well.

Tip

Choose sweet potatoes that are straight and not too thick, as they will work better in your spiralizer.

3. Return cauliflower to the bowl and stir in flax mixture, goat cheese, garlic, basil, oregano and salt until well blended. Shape into a ball.

4. On prepared baking sheet, press cauliflower ball out into a 1/4-inch (0.5 cm) thick circle. Bake in preheated oven for 12 to 15 minutes or until golden brown. Remove from oven, leaving oven on, and let cool completely.

5. *Toppings:* Spread cream cheese over crust. Sprinkle nutmeg over cream cheese.

6. Using a spiralizer, cut sweet potatoes into thin strands.

7. In a medium skillet, heat oil over medium heat. Add sweet potatoes and cook, stirring, for 4 to 6 minutes or until just tender. Using tongs, layer sweet potatoes evenly over cream cheese.

8. In a bowl, using a fork, combine pecans, brown sugar, flour and butter. Sprinkle evenly over sweet potatoes.

9. Bake for 10 minutes or until hot and bubbling. Let cool for 3 minutes or until cheese is set. Cut into slices and serve.

Zucchini and Carrot Wrap with Creamy Avocado

If you love wraps, you will delight in the creamy goodness of avocado paired with crunchy vegetables in a wrap that is delectable, satisfying and great for a summer picnic.

MAKES 4 SERVINGS

Tips

To wrap your tortilla so it holds in all of your delicious ingredients, fold the left and right sides of the tortilla into the middle until they are almost touching. Start rolling from the side closest to you, tucking in the ends, and keep rolling until fully rolled.

To make your wrap easier to eat, especially if you are on the go, place a piece of parchment or waxed paper under the tortilla before filling it. After rolling the tortilla, wrap the paper around the roll. Cut it in half through the paper. Peel back the paper as you eat.

3	carrots, peeled and ends cut flat	3
2	zucchini, ends cut flat	2
½ cup	hummus	125 mL
4	6- to 8-inch (15 to 20 cm) flour tortillas	4
1	avocado, sliced	1
	Kosher salt (optional)	
	Freshly ground black pepper (optional)	
1 cup	rinsed drained canned black beans	250 mL
3 tbsp	crumbled feta cheese or Vegan Feta (see tip, page 137)	45 mL

1. Using a spiralizer, cut carrots and zucchini into fine strands.

2. Spread hummus evenly over tortillas, leaving a ¾-inch (2 cm) border. Top with avocado slices. If desired, season to taste with salt and pepper. Layer with carrots, zucchini and beans. Sprinkle with feta. Roll up and secure with toothpicks. Cut each roll in half on the diagonal.

Glazed Spiral Fruit and Veggies

Here, the holy grail of cinnamon, apples and carrots is glazed with a buttery orange syrup that makes for a colorful and flavorful side dish.

Tips

You can trim the apple and carrot strands into shorter lengths, if desired. Doing so will give this dish a slaw-like appearance.

While I have a hard time waiting to dig in to this salad, it does get better the longer it stands. It is great for a make-ahead salad: prepare it a day in advance, cover and refrigerate, freeing up your time for other dishes or spending time with friends and family.

¼ cup	butter	60 mL
¼ cup	orange juice	60 mL
3 tbsp	pure maple syrup	45 mL
1 tsp	ground cinnamon	5 mL
4	carrots, peeled and ends cut flat	4
3	sweet apples (such as Gala or Jonagold), cored and ends cut flat	3
½ cup	raisins	125 mL
½ cup	chopped walnuts	125 mL

1. In a small saucepan, melt butter over medium heat. Stir in orange juice, maple syrup and cinnamon. Remove from heat and let cool.

2. Using a spiralizer, cut carrots and apples into thin strands.

3. In a serving bowl, combine carrots, apples, raisins, walnuts and orange-maple glaze, tossing to combine. Let stand for 15 minutes to blend the flavors.

No-Knead Roasted Squash Focaccia

This quick and easy version of focaccia will delight your senses with the crispy sweetness of squash and the intriguing flavors of herbs.

MAKES 1 LOAF

Tip

The bulbous end of the butternut squash contains seeds, so it does not spiralize well. Try roasting it instead, for a luscious side dish with any meal. Peel the squash, remove seeds and cut into 1½-inch (4 cm) cubes. Toss with melted butter, brown sugar, salt and pepper and roast in a 400°F (200°C) oven for 20 to 25 minutes.

▸ **10-inch (25 cm) ovenproof skillet, coated with 3 tbsp (45 mL) olive oil**
▸ **Rimmed baking sheet, lined with foil**

2½ cups	whole wheat flour	625 mL
	Kosher salt	
⅜ tsp	active dry yeast	1.5 mL
1 cup + 2 tbsp	water	275 mL
1	butternut squash neck (at least 4 inches/10 cm long)	1
3 tbsp	olive oil, divided	45 mL
	Freshly cracked black pepper	
2 tsp	chopped fresh rosemary	10 mL
	Liquid honey	
1½ tbsp	chopped fresh thyme	22 mL

1. In a large bowl, combine flour, 2 tsp (10 mL) salt and yeast. Add water and mix thoroughly using your hands. Cover the bowl tightly with plastic wrap and let rise at room temperature for 18 hours or until surface is bubbly. The dough will be at least three to four times its original size.

2. Sprinkle dough lightly with flour and, using your hands, fold dough over onto itself, rotating it to form a compact ball. Place dough in prepared skillet. Using your hands, spread dough to cover bottom of skillet. Flip dough to cover both sides with oil. Cover with a kitchen towel and let stand at room temperature for 2 hours.

After the rise in step 1, you can store the dough, wrapped tightly in plastic wrap, in the refrigerator for up to 3 days. Let stand, covered, for 2 hours at room temperature before continuing with step 2.

3. Preheat oven to 400°F (200°C), with the rack in the middle position.

4. Peel squash necks and trim to 4 inches (10 cm) long, with flat ends. Using a spiralizer, cut squash into wide ribbons.

5. In a large bowl, toss squash, 2 tbsp (30 mL) oil, and salt and pepper to taste until evenly coated.

6. Spread squash on prepared baking sheet and bake for 15 minutes or until tender. Remove from oven and let cool completely. Increase oven temperature to 450°F (230°C).

7. Press cooled squash into the dough. Sprinkle with rosemary. Brush with the remaining oil.

8. Bake for 25 to 30 minutes or until golden brown. Let cool for 5 minutes. Drizzle lightly with honey to taste. Sprinkle with thyme and salt to taste. Serve warm.

Green Beans with Crispy Spiral Onions

Borrowing the anchor ingredients of the classic holiday side dish, this version, with a refreshing Dijon vinaigrette, is suited for warmer weather.

Tip

Choose onions that are firm and dry and have a lustrous outer skin. Onions have a tendency to spray some juice while they are being spiralized. Take care to protect your eyes and other surfaces.

▸ **Preheat oven to 425°F (220°C)**

▸ **Rimmed baking sheet, lined with foil**

1	red onion, peeled and ends cut flat	1
1 tbsp	olive oil	15 mL
	Seasoned salt	
1 lb	tender green beans, trimmed	500 g
	Ice water	
2 tbsp	butter or virgin coconut oil	30 mL
8 oz	cremini mushrooms, thinly sliced	250 g

Dijon Vinaigrette

6 tbsp	extra virgin olive oil	90 mL
2½ tbsp	white wine vinegar	37 mL
1 tbsp	Dijon mustard	15 mL
Pinch	kosher salt	Pinch
Pinch	freshly ground black pepper	Pinch

1. Using a spiralizer, cut onion into thin strands.

2. Place onion on prepared baking sheet, drizzle with oil and season to taste with seasoned salt. Toss to coat, then separate strands so they are not touching. Bake in preheated oven for 15 to 20 minutes, tossing occasionally, until crispy.

Tip

The vinaigrette recipe is easily doubled and will keep for up to 2 weeks in the refrigerator. When ready to use, bring it to room temperature and shake to combine.

3. Meanwhile, in a pot of boiling water, cook beans for 2 to 3 minutes or until tender-crisp. Using a slotted spoon, immediately transfer beans to a bowl of ice water. Drain beans thoroughly and pat dry.

4. In a medium skillet, melt butter over medium heat. Add mushrooms and cook, stirring, for 5 to 7 minutes or until lightly browned. Add beans and cook, stirring, for 1 minute or until heated through. Using a slotted spoon, transfer mushrooms and beans to a serving bowl.

5. *Vinaigrette:* In a small jar with a tight-fitting lid, combine oil, vinegar, mustard, salt and pepper. Cover tightly and shake to combine.

6. Add vinaigrette to beans and mushrooms, tossing to combine. Top with crispy onions.

Ribbon Potato Leek Gratin

A trio of potatoes, celery root and leeks topped with a creamy sauce and a crispy topping makes for a captivating dish.

Tips

Leeks are grown packed in sandy soil and retain this soil right into your kitchen. To clean them, cut the root ends and green tops off. Trim to 4-inch (10 cm) sections, then slice down the full length of the leek. Separate the sections and add to a large bowl filled with cold water. Using your fingers, rinse off any remaining dirt. The leeks will float and the dirt will fall to the bottom. Pat dry before slicing.

Choose russet potatoes that are straight and not too thick, as they will work better in your spiralizer.

▸ **Preheat oven to 350°F (180°C)**

▸ **11- by 7-inch (28 by 18 cm) glass baking dish, greased**

3½ tbsp	olive oil, divided	52 mL
3	leeks (white and light green parts only), thinly sliced	3
3	cloves garlic, minced	3
4	fresh thyme sprigs	4
½ tsp	kosher salt	2 mL
¼ tsp	freshly ground black pepper	1 mL
1 cup	coconut milk	250 mL
1 cup	ready-to-use reduced-sodium vegetable broth	250 mL
3	russet potatoes, peeled and ends cut flat	3
2	small celery roots, peeled and ends cut flat	2
¼ cup	nutritional yeast	60 mL
3 tbsp	Italian-seasoned bread crumbs	45 mL

1. In a large skillet, heat 2 tbsp (30 mL) oil over medium-high heat. Add leeks, separating rings, and cook, stirring, for 7 to 9 minutes or until soft and translucent. Transfer one-third of the leeks to a plate lined with paper towels.

2. Add garlic to the leeks remaining in the skillet and cook, stirring, for 30 seconds or until fragrant. Reduce heat to medium and add thyme, salt, pepper, coconut milk and broth. Cook, stirring, for 8 to 10 minutes or until reduced by one-third. Discard thyme.

Tip

Use a paring knife to peel the skin off the celery roots. You want to cut down to the creamy white flesh, removing the skin and darker internal layer. Depending on the size or awkward shape of your celery roots, you may want to cut the roots in half. Keep in mind that they need to fit in your spiralizer.

3. Meanwhile, using a spiralizer, cut potatoes and celery roots into wide ribbons.

4. Place half of the potato and celery root ribbons in prepared baking dish. Drizzle with half of the leek sauce. Repeat with the remaining ribbons and sauce. Cover with foil.

5. Bake in preheated oven for 25 minutes.

6. Meanwhile, in a small bowl, combine yeast, bread crumbs and the remaining oil.

7. Remove foil and sprinkle potato mixture with bread crumb mixture and the reserved leeks. Bake for 5 to 10 minutes or until top is browned and edges are bubbling. Let cool slightly before cutting.

Spicy Shoestring Jicama Fries

Jicama makes a unique, sweet and crispy shoestring fry that is a wonderful alternative to potato fries or absolutely tantalizing as a midday or after-school snack.

Tip

Lining your baking sheets with foil makes cleaning them much easier. You could also use just one baking sheet and bake the jicama in batches, replacing the foil between batches.

► **Preheat oven to 400°F (200°C), with one rack in the upper third and one in the bottom third**

► **Rimmed baking sheets, lined with foil**

1	large jicama, peeled and ends cut flat	1
2 tbsp	olive oil	30 mL
1 tbsp	onion powder	15 mL
2 tsp	Hungarian paprika	10 mL
2 tsp	kosher salt	10 mL
1 tsp	ground cumin	5 mL

1. Using a spiralizer, cut jicama into medium strands. Trim strands to 6-inch (15 cm) lengths and pat dry.

2. Divide jicama between prepared baking sheets. Drizzle with oil and season with onion powder, paprika, salt and cumin. Toss to coat evenly, then spread out jicama so strands are not touching.

3. Place one baking sheet in the upper third of the preheated oven and the other in the bottom third. Bake for 6 minutes. Pull out baking sheets and turn jicama strands. Return to the oven, swapping the sheets' positions on the racks. Bake for 4 to 10 minutes or until cooked to desired tenderness. Serve immediately.

Raw Food Recipes

Crispy Cabbage and Fennel Slaw

You will enjoy diving in to the crunch of sweet carrots, tart apples, earthy cabbage and the delightful hint of licorice, melded together with a citrus mustard vinaigrette.

Tip

You can substitute 1 tbsp (15 mL) minced gingerroot for the shallot if you want the salad to have a little bit more bite.

2	carrots, peeled and ends cut flat	2
2	tart apples (such as Braeburn or Pink Lady), cored and ends cut flat	2
1	small head red cabbage, outer leaves removed and ends cut flat	1
1	fennel bulb, ends cut flat	1
1	shallot, finely chopped	1
1 tsp	dry mustard	5 mL
½ cup	cold-pressed hemp oil	125 mL
3 tbsp	freshly squeezed orange juice	45 mL
1 tbsp	cider vinegar	15 mL
	Kosher salt	
	Freshly ground black pepper	

1. Using a spiralizer, cut carrots, apples, cabbage and fennel into medium strands. Trim all strands to desired length. Transfer to a large bowl.

2. In a jar with a tight-fitting lid, combine shallot, mustard, hemp oil, orange juice and vinegar. Cover tightly and shake vigorously to combine.

3. Drizzle dressing over carrot mixture and toss to coat. Cover and refrigerate for at least 1 hour, until chilled, or for up to 3 hours. Season to taste with salt and pepper. Toss to combine.

Creamy Carrot and Cabbage Slaw

If you crave the childhood peanut butter days, you will find pleasure in the slightly sweet and salty flavors that flow from the creamy peanut dressing that baths crunchy cabbage, carrots and radishes.

**MAKES
4 SERVINGS**

Tip

Depending on the size of your cabbage and spiralizer, you may need to cut the cabbage in half to make it easier to spiralize.

4	carrots, peeled and ends cut flat	4
4	large red radishes, ends cut flat	4
1	small head green cabbage, outer leaves removed and ends cut flat	1
3 tbsp	raw creamy peanut butter	45 mL
3 tbsp	rice vinegar	45 mL
2 tbsp	freshly squeezed lemon juice	30 mL
2 tbsp	cold-pressed extra virgin olive oil	30 mL
1 tbsp	tamari	15 mL
¼ cup	chopped raw peanuts	60 mL

1. Using a spiralizer, cut carrots, radishes and cabbage into fine strands. Transfer to a large bowl.

2. In a small bowl, whisk together peanut butter, vinegar, lemon juice, oil and tamari.

3. Drizzle dressing over cabbage mixture and toss to combine. Cover and refrigerate for at least 1 hour, until chilled, or for up to 3 hours. Just before serving, sprinkle with peanuts.

Multicolor Slaw with Peanut Lime Dressing

A bounty of vegetables is topped by a sassy dressing that will awaken all of your taste buds.

MAKES 6 TO 8 SERVINGS

Tip

The peanut lime dressing is easy to double and can be stored in an airtight container in the refrigerator for up to 1 week. It works well on a variety of salads and is a wonderful dipping sauce for veggies.

▶ **Blender**

2	carrots, peeled and ends cut flat	2
1	head green cabbage, cut in half, outer leaves peeled and ends cut flat	1
1	jicama, peeled and ends cut flat	1
1	beet, peeled and ends cut flat	1
1	daikon radish, peeled and ends cut flat	1
3	cloves garlic, coarsely chopped	3
2 tbsp	chopped fresh cilantro	30 mL
2 tsp	finely chopped gingerroot	10 mL
3 tbsp	freshly squeezed lime juice	45 mL
2 tbsp	raw creamy peanut butter	30 mL
1 tbsp	tamari	15 mL
1 tbsp	cider vinegar	15 mL
2 tsp	coconut milk	10 mL
1 tsp	cold-pressed sesame oil	5 mL
½ cup	cold-pressed sunflower oil	125 mL
¼ cup	chopped unsalted raw peanuts	60 mL

1. Using a spiralizer, cut carrots, cabbage, jicama, beet and radish into medium strands. Pat jicama strands dry. Transfer to a large bowl.

2. In a blender, combine garlic, cilantro, ginger, lime juice, peanut butter, tamari, vinegar, coconut milk and sesame oil; blend until smooth. With the motor running, through the feed tube, gradually add sunflower oil, blending until smooth.

3. Drizzle dressing over carrot mixture and toss to coat. Let stand for 15 minutes. Sprinkle with peanuts.

Kohlrabi Slaw

This easy slaw is a great way to try crisp, sweet, delectable kohlrabi.

Tip

This salad is so versatile you can serve it as a starter, side dish or light lunch. If you want to eat it as a main course, add the sprouted amaranth for a punch of protein.

▶ **Mortar and pestle**

3	kohlrabi, peeled and ends cut flat	3
2	carrots, peeled and ends cut flat	2
2	sweet apples (such as Gala or Jonagold), cored and ends cut flat	2
1	clove garlic, coarsely chopped	1
1 tsp	kosher salt	5 mL
1 tsp	dry mustard	5 mL
½ tsp	celery seeds	2 mL
Pinch	freshly ground black pepper	Pinch
3 tbsp	freshly squeezed lemon juice	45 mL
2 tbsp	cold-pressed sesame oil	30 mL
1 tbsp	cider vinegar	15 mL
⅔ cup	sprouted amaranth (optional)	150 mL

1. Using a spiralizer, cut kohlrabi, carrots and apples into thin strands. Transfer to a large bowl.

2. Using a mortar and pestle, grind garlic and salt into a fine paste. Transfer to a small bowl and whisk in mustard, celery seeds, pepper, lemon juice, oil and vinegar.

3. Drizzle dressing over kohlrabi mixture and toss to combine. Top with amaranth (if using).

Sprouted Amaranth

You can either purchase sprouted amaranth or sprout it yourself. To sprout it at home, you will need to plan ahead, as the process can take up to 2 days. Add ½ cup (125 mL) amaranth seeds and 1 cup (250 mL) water to a 1-quart (1 L) canning jar. Cover the jar with fine-mesh cheesecloth, affixing it tightly with the screw band of the jar or a rubber band, and let stand in a cool, undisturbed place for at least 12 hours. Drain the water, rinse the amaranth with fresh water and drain again. Return the amaranth to the jar and make sure there is no standing water in the jar. Cover the jar with fine-mesh cheesecloth, affixing it tightly. Place the jar on its side or at an angle so that air can circulate inside. Store in a cool, mostly dark place. Continue draining and rinsing the amaranth every 12 hours until sprouts appear and are the desired length.

Lively Brussels Sprout Almond Salad

The blissful marriage of Brussels sprouts, apples and celery root is made even more mouthwatering with a refreshing lemon thyme vinaigrette in this robust salad.

Tip

While Brussels sprouts often get a bad rap, these little green gems are wonderful if you choose sprouts that are less than 1½ inches (4 cm) in diameter. Smaller sprouts have a much sweeter taste. They should also be firm and green, with compact leaves. Slice them as thin as possible to allow the vinaigrette to work its magic.

▶ **Mortar and pestle**

1	clove garlic, coarsely chopped	1
2 tbsp	coarsely chopped shallots	30 mL
1 tsp	mustard seeds	5 mL
1 tbsp	chopped fresh thyme	15 mL
¼ cup	cold-pressed extra virgin olive oil	60 mL
2 tbsp	freshly squeezed lemon juice	30 mL
2	crisp apples (such as Red or Golden Delicious), cored and ends cut flat	2
1	celery root, peeled and ends cut flat	1
8 oz	Brussels sprouts, trimmed and thinly sliced	250 g
¼ cup	sliced raw almonds	60 mL

1. Using a mortar and pestle, grind garlic, shallots and mustard seeds to a paste. Transfer to a small bowl and whisk in thyme, oil and lemon juice. Set aside.

2. Using a spiralizer, cut apples and celery root into medium strands.

3. In a large bowl, combine apples, celery root and Brussels sprouts. Drizzle with dressing and toss to combine. Refrigerate for at least 1 hour or up to 3 hours to blend the flavors and soften vegetables. Just before serving, add almonds and toss to combine.

Curly Cucumber Greek Salad

The Mediterranean comes to life with the refreshing flavors of this delightful salad. Serve as a main dish or as a side — either way, you are sure to enjoy it.

**MAKES
3 SERVINGS**

Tips

Cashew Feta: In a small food processor, combine ½ cup (125 mL) raw cashews, 1 tbsp (15 mL) extra virgin olive oil and 1½ tsp (7 mL) dried oregano; process to a consistency similar to crumbled feta.

This recipe can easily be expanded for as many servings as you would like.

2	cucumbers, ends cut flat	2
1	small red onion, peeled and ends cut flat	1
¾ cup	cherry tomatoes, cut in half	175 mL
⅓ cup	kalamata olives, pitted	75 mL
3 tbsp	chopped fresh parsley	45 mL
2 tbsp	cold-pressed extra virgin olive oil	30 mL
1½ tbsp	red wine vinegar	22 mL
1 tsp	chopped fresh oregano	5 mL
½ cup	Cashew Feta (optional; see tip, at left)	125 mL
	Freshly ground black pepper (optional)	

1. Using a spiralizer, cut cucumbers and onion into medium strands. Pat cucumber strands dry.

2. In a large bowl, combine cucumbers, onion, tomatoes, olives and parsley. Drizzle oil and vinegar evenly over top. Sprinkle with fresh oregano. Toss gently to combine. If desired, sprinkle with Cashew Feta and pepper.

Divine Greek Salad

You'll feel the kiss of the Mediterranean sun when you taste this bounty of fresh vegetables and a quintessential Greek vinaigrette.

**MAKES
6 SERVINGS**

Tip

If sun-ripened tomatoes are not available, you can use organic or heirloom tomatoes.

2	cucumbers, ends cut flat	2
1	small red onion, peeled and ends cut flat	1
1	small green bell pepper, stem removed	1
4	sun-ripened tomatoes, cored and cut into sixths	4
1 cup	sprouted lentils (see box, below)	250 mL
¼ cup	torn fresh oregano (optional)	60 mL
2	cloves garlic, minced	2
¼ tsp	kosher salt	1 mL
Pinch	dry mustard	Pinch
½ cup	cold-pressed extra virgin olive oil	125 mL
¼ cup	red wine vinegar	60 mL

1. Using a spiralizer, cut cucumbers into wide ribbons and pat dry. Cut onion and green pepper into medium strands. Remove white flesh and seeds from pepper. Trim all ribbons and strands to desired length.

2. In a large bowl, combine spiralized vegetables, tomatoes, lentils and oregano (if using).

3. In a small bowl, whisk together garlic, salt, mustard, oil and vinegar.

4. Drizzle dressing over salad and toss to combine.

Sprouted Lentils

You can either purchase sprouted lentils or sprout them yourself. To sprout them at home, you will need to plan ahead, as the process can take up to 4 days. Add ⅓ cup (75 mL) dried lentils and 1 cup (250 mL) water to a 1-quart (1 L) canning jar. Cover the jar with fine-mesh cheesecloth, affixing it tightly with the screw band of the jar or a rubber band, and let stand in a cool, undisturbed place for at least 12 hours. Drain the water, rinse the lentils with fresh water and drain again. Return the lentils to the jar and make sure there is no standing water in the jar. Cover the jar with fine-mesh cheesecloth, affixing it tightly. Place the jar on its side or at an angle so that air can circulate inside. Store in a cool, mostly dark place. Continue draining and rinsing the lentils every 12 hours until sprouts appear and are the desired length.

Cucumber Noodles with Spicy Sesame Dressing

This crispy, cool and spicy salad is satisfying as a starter or a side dish.

Tips

Cucumbers have a high water content. Pat the ribbons dry as much as possible before adding them to your salad. You can also sprinkle them lightly with salt, place them in a colander and let them drain for 15 minutes (or while you are preparing the other ingredients).

When spiralizing, you always end up with a little bit of vegetable or fruit that is too small to spiralize. I use these pieces to taste-test my dressing before adding it to the salad.

4	cucumbers, ends cut flat	4
2	carrots, peeled and ends cut flat	2
2	cloves garlic, minced	2
2 tsp	grated gingerroot	10 mL
1/4 cup	tamari	60 mL
1 tbsp	freshly squeezed lime juice	15 mL
1 tbsp	cold-pressed sesame oil	15 mL
1 1/2 tsp	rice vinegar	7 mL
1 to 2 tsp	raw hot pepper sauce	5 to 10 mL
1 tsp	raw liquid honey	5 mL
Pinch	hot pepper flakes	Pinch
	Torn fresh cilantro leaves (optional)	

1. Using a spiralizer, cut cucumbers and carrots into thin strands. Pat cucumber strands dry. Transfer to a large bowl.

2. In a small bowl, whisk together garlic, ginger, tamari, lime juice, oil, vinegar, hot pepper sauce to taste and honey.

3. Drizzle dressing over cucumber mixture and toss to combine. Sprinkle with hot pepper flakes and cilantro (if using).

Sicilian Corkscrew Zucchini Salad

This refreshing, colorful salad is a delicious starter or appetizer. It is reminiscent of those long, hot summers when you enjoyed biting into a melon and letting the juice roll down your chin.

Tips

To make this dish fun for kids (and you) to prepare and eat, swirl the zucchini strands into small nest-like shapes on the serving plates. Add the melon balls and tomatoes to the center of the nests.

To make the zucchini strands easier to eat, cut them into roughly 10-inch (25 cm) lengths.

▶ **Small ice cream scoop or melon baller**

3	zucchini, ends cut flat	3
1 cup	packed fresh basil, coarsely chopped	250 mL
2 tsp	kosher salt	10 mL
¼ cup	cold-pressed extra virgin olive oil	60 mL
1½ tbsp	white wine vinegar	22 mL
1	white melon (such as Canary or Gaya), halved and seeded	1
1 cup	cherry tomatoes, halved	250 mL
	Hot pepper flakes (optional)	
	Kosher salt (optional)	
	Balsamic vinegar (optional)	

1. Using a spiralizer, cut zucchini into thin strands. Transfer to a large bowl.
2. In a small bowl, whisk together basil, salt, oil and white wine vinegar.
3. Drizzle half the dressing over zucchini and toss to combine. Divide among four serving plates.
4. Using a small ice cream scoop, cut melon into small balls.
5. Add melon balls and tomatoes to zucchini. Drizzle with the remaining dressing. If desired, sprinkle with hot pepper flakes, salt and/or balsamic vinegar.

Tangy Zucchini, Apple and Walnut Salad

The cranberry dressing adds just the right amount of punch to this combination of zucchini, sweet apples and earthy walnuts.

MAKES 6 SERVINGS

Tip

If you prefer not to use balsamic vinegar, you can substitute freshly squeezed orange juice and eliminate the agave nectar (or add it to taste).

▶ **Food processor**

¼ cup	fresh or thawed frozen cranberries	60 mL
½ tsp	dry mustard	2 mL
3 tbsp	balsamic vinegar	45 mL
1 tbsp	raw agave nectar	15 mL
⅔ cup	cold-pressed extra virgin olive oil	150 mL
	Kosher salt	
4	zucchini, ends cut flat	4
2	crisp apples (such as Red or Golden Delicious), cored and ends cut flat	2
½	small red onion, peeled and ends cut flat (optional)	½
3 cups	packed mesclun mix or mixed baby greens	750 mL
½ cup	chopped raw walnuts	125 mL

1. In food processor, process cranberries until finely chopped. Add mustard, vinegar and agave nectar; process until smooth. With the motor running, through the feed tube, gradually add oil, processing until emulsified. Season to taste with salt. Set aside.

2. Using a spiralizer, cut zucchini, apples and onion (if using) into thin strands. Transfer to a large bowl.

3. Add mesclun mix and dressing to zucchini mixture and toss to combine. Sprinkle with walnuts.

Spiralized Zucchini Salad with Avocado and Tomatoes

The freshness of summer's bounty shines through in this salad of zucchini and tomatoes graced with a basil vinaigrette that lets the true flavors shine through.

Tip

This mustard vinaigrette makes a wonderful base for a variety of herbs. Instead of basil, you may want to try fresh parsley, cilantro or thyme. You will need about ¼ cup (60 mL) parsley or cilantro, or about 2 tbsp (30 mL) thyme.

▶ **Blender**

4	zucchini, ends cut flat	4
15	basil leaves	15
2	cloves garlic, coarsely chopped	2
2 tsp	kosher salt	10 mL
2 tsp	dry mustard	10 mL
2 tbsp	balsamic vinegar	30 mL
2 tsp	freshly squeezed lemon juice	10 mL
⅓ cup	cold-pressed hemp oil	75 mL
2	avocados, cubed	2
1½ cups	cherry tomatoes, halved	375 mL

1. Using a spiralizer, cut zucchini into medium strands. Trim strands to 10 inches (25 cm) long. Transfer to a large bowl.

2. In blender, combine basil, garlic, salt, mustard, vinegar and lemon juice; pulse to combine. With the motor running, through the feed tube, gradually add oil, blending until combined.

3. Drizzle dressing over zucchini and gently toss to combine. Top with avocados and tomatoes.

Curried Zucchini Noodle Salad with Tomatoes and Mango

This delightful salad adds a spectrum of spicy seasonings to cooling vegetables and fruits.

Tip

To choose a perfectly ripened mango, squeeze it gently to check if it gives slightly. Do not choose a mango by color, as some varieties display a spectrum of red to yellow colors. Occasionally, the base of the stem will have a fruity aroma.

2	zucchini, ends cut flat	2
2 tsp	freshly squeezed lime juice	10 mL
2 tsp	white vinegar	10 mL
2 tsp	red curry paste	10 mL
1 tsp	sesame oil	5 mL
Pinch	kosher salt	Pinch
4 cups	packed mesclun mix or mixed baby greens	1 L
½ cup	cherry tomatoes, halved	125 mL
1	mango, cut into 1-inch (2.5 cm) cubes	1
	Torn fresh cilantro (optional)	
	Hot pepper flakes (optional)	

1. Using a spiralizer, cut zucchini into thin strands. Trim strands to desired length. Transfer to a medium bowl.

2. In a small bowl, whisk together lime juice, vinegar, curry paste, oil and salt. Drizzle half the dressing over zucchini strands and toss to coat.

3. Arrange mesclun mix, tomatoes and mango on individual salad plates. Using tongs, arrange zucchini mixture on top. If desired, sprinkle with cilantro and hot pepper flakes. Serve with the remaining dressing on the side.

Variation

For complete Thai-inspired flavor, replace the salt with dulse flakes.

Zucchini Pasta with Velvety Tomato Sauce

This cool dressing will become one your favorites thanks to its vibrant flavors and velvety finish. I like to add a light green salad with a lemon basil vinaigrette as a preface to this main dish.

MAKES 3 TO 4 SERVINGS

Tips

You can leave the zucchini unpeeled if you prefer to have the nutrients from the skin or to save time.

To make peeling tomatoes easier without losing too much flesh, cut the tomatoes into wedges first. Place the wedges skin side down on a cutting board. Using a very sharp knife, start at one end of the wedge and cut slowly in a downward motion, holding the peel as you cut.

To soak the sun-dried tomatoes, place them in a bowl and cover with 1 cup (250 mL) warm water. Let stand for 20 minutes. Drain liquid before adding to blender.

▶ **Blender**

4	zucchini, peeled (see tip, at left) and ends cut flat	4
3	tomatoes, cut into wedges and peeled	3
2	cloves garlic, coarsely chopped	2
¼ cup	sun-dried tomatoes, soaked (see tip at left)	60 mL
¼ cup	chopped green bell pepper	60 mL
3 tbsp	packed fresh basil (about 12 leaves)	45 mL
½ tsp	dried oregano	2 mL
¼ tsp	kosher salt	1 mL
1 tbsp	freshly squeezed lemon juice	15 mL
¼ cup	cold-pressed extra virgin olive oil	60 mL
4 oz	mushrooms, sliced	125 g
	Hot pepper flakes (optional)	
	Nutritional yeast (optional)	

1. Using a spiralizer, cut zucchini into thin strands. Transfer to a large bowl.

2. In blender, combine tomato wedges, garlic, sun-dried tomatoes, green pepper, basil, oregano, salt and lemon juice; blend until smooth. With the motor running, through the feed tube, gradually add oil, blending until emulsified. Add mushrooms and pulse until slightly chunky.

3. Pour sauce over zucchini. If desired, sprinkle with hot pepper flakes and nutritional yeast.

Zucchini Pasta with Pine Nuts and Cranberries

You will be pleasantly surprised by the tantalizing influences that raw Caesar dressing and cranberries add to garden-fresh zucchini noodles.

MAKES 4 TO 5 SERVINGS

Tip

Dulse is a sea vegetable harvested in the cold waters of the North Atlantic and then dried. Dulse flakes add a tangy, slightly salty flavor to this dish.

▶ **Blender**

1	clove garlic, coarsely chopped	1
⅓ cup	raw pine nuts	75 mL
1½ tbsp	dulse flakes	22 mL
1 tbsp	chopped fresh basil	15 mL
3 tbsp	water	45 mL
2 tsp	freshly squeezed orange juice	10 mL
1 tsp	freshly squeezed lemon juice	5 mL
5	zucchini, ends cut flat	5
	Kosher salt	
	Freshly ground black pepper	
½ cup	dried cranberries	125 mL
	Hot pepper flakes (optional)	

1. In blender, combine garlic, pine nuts, dulse flakes, basil, water, orange juice and lemon juice; blend until smooth. Refrigerate for 30 minutes.

2. Meanwhile, using a spiralizer, cut zucchini into medium strands. Transfer to a large bowl.

3. Remove dressing from refrigerator and thin to desired consistency with water, if necessary. Season to taste with salt and pepper.

4. Add cranberries to zucchini. Drizzle with dressing and toss to combine. Sprinkle with hot pepper flakes (if using).

Crunchy Veggie Salad with Miso Ginger Dressing

This crispy blend of vegetables on a bed of escarole is finished with a sweet and savory citrus dressing that adds a new level of satisfying flavors.

MAKES 4 SERVINGS

Tips

While brown rice miso is not considered a raw food, it is often used in raw cuisine because it is gluten-free, adds distinctive flavor and aids in digestion because it is fermented.

Wear gloves when working with red beets so they don't stain your hands. Wash your spiralizer immediately after cutting beets to avoid discoloration.

2	carrots, peeled and ends cut flat	2
2	turnips, peeled and ends cut flat	2
2	red beets, peeled and ends cut flat	2
½ tsp	minced gingerroot	2 mL
¼ cup	brown rice miso (see tip, at left)	60 mL
3 tbsp	water	45 mL
1 tbsp	cold-pressed sesame oil	15 mL
1 tbsp	freshly squeezed orange juice	15 mL
1 tsp	raw liquid honey	5 mL
2 cups	packed escarole	500 mL
½ cup	chopped raw walnuts	125 mL

1. Using a spiralizer, cut carrots, turnips and beets into thin strands. Transfer to a large bowl.

2. In a small bowl, whisk together ginger, miso, water, oil, orange juice and honey.

3. Drizzle dressing over carrot mixture and toss to coat. Let stand for 10 minutes to blend the flavors and soften vegetables slightly.

4. Divide escarole among four serving plates. Top with salad and sprinkle with walnuts.

Squiggly Summer Vegetables

The colorful array of vegetables, with their varied tastes and textures, is especially scrumptious with a lemon mustard vinaigrette and crunchy sunflower seeds.

**MAKES
6 SERVINGS**

Variations

Use ¼ cup (60 mL) raw green pumpkin seeds (pepitas) in place of the sunflower seeds.

Dried cranberries or cherries add a nice tart finish to this salad. Add ¼ cup (60 mL) or more, to taste, just before the final toss.

Cold-pressed hemp oil can be used in place of the olive oil.

▶ **Mortar and pestle**

2	large radishes, ends cut flat	2
2	red or yellow beets, peeled and ends cut flat	2
2	carrots, peeled and ends cut flat	2
2	yellow summer squash, ends cut flat	2
2	stalks celery, chopped	2
1	shallot, minced	1
1	clove garlic, minced	1
½ tsp	kosher salt	2 mL
2 tsp	dry mustard	10 mL
⅓ cup	cold-pressed extra virgin olive oil	75 mL
3 tbsp	freshly squeezed lemon juice	45 mL
1 cup	packed arugula	250 mL
½ cup	raw sunflower seeds	125 mL

1. Using a spiralizer, cut radishes into wide ribbons. Cut beets, carrots and squash into thin strands and trim strands to 8-inch (20 cm) lengths.

2. In a large bowl, combine spiralized vegetables and celery. Set aside.

3. Using a mortar and pestle, mash shallot, garlic and salt into a paste. Transfer to a small bowl and whisk in mustard, oil and lemon juice.

4. Drizzle dressing over salad and toss to combine. Let stand for at least 30 minutes, to blend the flavors, or for up to 3 hours. Just before serving, add arugula and sunflower seeds, tossing to combine.

Kaleidoscope Salad

This salad kick-starts your senses with its curly, colorful, ever-changing textures, sweet and savory flavors and delectable crunchy topping.

MAKES 6 SERVINGS

Tips

After spiralizing bell peppers, you will need to remove the white flesh and seeds from the strands. Alternatively, you can core the peppers, but they will not hold their shape as well during spiralizing.

The salad topping can be used on a variety of fruit and vegetable dishes. It can be prepared ahead of time and stored in an airtight container in the refrigerator for up to 1 month.

▶ **Blender**

Salad Base

2	carrots, peeled and ends cut flat	2
2	parsnips, peeled and ends cut flat	2
1	jicama, peeled and ends cut flat	1
1	cucumber, ends cut flat	1
1	green bell pepper, stem removed (see tip, at left)	1
1	small red onion, ends cut flat	1
3 cups	watercress	750 mL
2	tomatoes, cut into wedges	2

Dressing

½ cup	fresh cilantro	125 mL
2 tbsp	fresh dill	30 mL
¼ cup	freshly squeezed orange juice	60 mL
2 tbsp	freshly squeezed lime juice	30 mL
2 tbsp	freshly squeezed lemon juice	30 mL
½ tsp	raw agave nectar	2 mL
¾ cup	cold-pressed extra virgin olive oil	175 mL
Pinch	kosher salt	Pinch

Topping

½ cup	sprouted quinoa (see box, opposite)	125 mL
½ cup	sun-dried goji berries	125 mL
¼ cup	sliced raw almonds	60 mL
¼ cup	chopped raw peanuts	60 mL
3 tbsp	chia seeds	45 mL
	Kosher salt (optional)	

1. *Salad Base:* Using a spiralizer, cut carrots, parsnips, jicama, cucumber, green pepper and onion into medium strands. Pat jicama and cucumber strands dry. Remove white flesh and seeds from pepper.

2. Place watercress in a large bowl. Add spiralized strands in random twisting layers on top. Top with tomato wedges.

3. *Dressing:* In blender, combine cilantro, dill, orange juice, lime juice, lemon juice and agave nectar. With the motor running, through the feed tube, gradually add oil, blending until emulsified. Season to taste with salt. Drizzle over salad.

4. *Topping:* In a medium bowl, combine quinoa, goji berries, almonds, peanuts and chia seeds. Season to taste with salt, if desired. Sprinkle over salad.

Sprouted Quinoa

You can either purchase sprouted quinoa or sprout it yourself. To sprout it at home, you will need to plan ahead, as the process can take up to 4 days. Add ¼ cup (60 mL) quinoa and 1 cup (250 mL) water to a 1-quart (1 L) canning jar. Cover the jar with fine-mesh cheesecloth, affixing it tightly with the screw band of the jar or a rubber band, and let stand in a cool, undisturbed place for at least 12 hours. Drain the water, rinse the quinoa with fresh water and drain again. Return the quinoa to the jar and make sure there is no standing water in the jar. Cover the jar with fine-mesh cheesecloth, affixing it tightly. Place the jar on its side or at an angle so that air can circulate inside. Store in a cool, mostly dark place. Continue draining and rinsing the quinoa every 12 hours until sprouts appear and are the desired length.

Twisted Rainbow Salad with Basil Garlic Dressing

Drizzled with a basil garlic dressing and sprinkled with pomegranate seeds, this salad is as tasty as its colorful twists of crisp vegetables and fruit imply.

MAKES 6 TO 8 SERVINGS

Tips

I leave the spiralized strands long for this salad because I enjoy the look of the rainbow-colored twists. But you can trim them into shorter lengths if you find those easier to eat.

In addition to patting the cucumbers dry, you can toss them in a colander with a pinch of salt and let them drain until ready to use. This will reduce the chances of your salad becoming watery (cucumbers have a very high water content).

4	carrots, peeled and ends cut flat	4
2	cucumbers, ends cut flat	2
2	beets, peeled and ends cut flat	2
2	green apples, cored and ends cut flat	2
½ cup	packed fresh basil leaves, coarsely chopped	125 mL
2 tbsp	minced garlic	30 mL
2 tbsp	nutritional yeast	30 mL
¼ cup	white wine vinegar	60 mL
½ cup	cold-pressed extra virgin olive oil	125 mL
½ cup	pomegranate seeds	125 mL

1. Using a spiralizer, cut carrots, cucumbers, beets and apples into medium strands. Pat cucumbers dry. Transfer all strands to a large bowl.

2. In a small bowl, whisk together basil, garlic, yeast and vinegar. Gradually whisk in oil until combined.

3. Drizzle dressing over carrot mixture and toss to coat. Sprinkle with pomegranate seeds.

Crunchy Kale and Curly Vegetable Salad

The salad boasts a creamy cucumber avocado dressing that adds fresh flavor depth to the sweet carrots, daikon radish and earthy kale.

MAKES 4 SERVINGS

Tips

Choose kale that is crisp and brightly colored. Select the smallest leaves you can find, as they will be less bitter.

To shred kale, roll a stack of 8 to 10 leaves into a tight roll. Using a sharp knife, cut the leaves crosswise, then fluff them open and separate the shreds.

▶ **Blender**

3	carrots, peeled and ends cut flat	3
1	daikon radish, peeled and ends cut flat	1
2 cups	packed curly kale, shredded (see tips, at left)	500 mL
2	cloves garlic, minced	2
1	cucumber, peeled and cut into small chunks	1
1	avocado, cut into wedges	1
½ cup	packed fresh mint leaves	125 mL
2 tsp	fresh dill	10 mL
1 tsp	kosher salt	5 mL
3 tbsp	freshly squeezed orange juice	45 mL
2 tsp	raw agave nectar	10 mL
¼ cup	cold-pressed hemp oil	60 mL

1. Using a spiralizer, cut carrots and radish into thin strands.
2. In a large bowl, combine carrots, radish and kale.
3. In blender, combine garlic, cucumber, avocado, mint, dill, salt, orange juice and agave nectar; blend until smooth. With the motor running, through the feed tube, gradually add oil, blending until emulsified.
4. Drizzle dressing over carrot mixture and toss to coat. Let stand for 10 minutes before serving.

Kale with Curlycue Carrots and Sunflower Seed Dressing

This substantial salad is packed with refreshing, crunchy, nutritious vegetables and seeds dressed up with a creamy and tangy dressing.

~~~~~~

**MAKES
4 SERVINGS**

Tip

This salad can be eaten immediately or refrigerated in an airtight container for up to 2 days. If you are making this salad ahead, wait to add the sunflower and hemp seeds until just before serving.

3	carrots, peeled and ends cut flat	3
1	small red onion, peeled and ends cut flat	1
1	yellow bell pepper, stem removed (see tip, page 202)	1
3 cups	packed curly kale, shredded (see tips, page 205)	750 mL
¼ cup	raw sunflower seeds	60 mL
3 tbsp	raw shelled hemp seeds	45 mL
2 tsp	dry mustard	10 mL
½ tsp	kosher salt	2 mL
3 tbsp	cold-pressed extra virgin olive oil	45 mL
1½ tbsp	cider vinegar	22 mL
	Fresh cracked black pepper (optional)	

1. Using a spiralizer, cut carrots, onion and yellow pepper into thin strands. Remove white flesh and seeds from pepper.

2. In a large bowl, combine spiralized vegetables, kale, sunflower seeds and hemp seeds.

3. In a small bowl, whisk together mustard, salt, oil and vinegar.

4. Drizzle dressing over kale mixture and toss to coat. Season to taste with pepper (if using).

Spiral Carrot Salad with Orange Tarragon Dressing

This refreshing salad bathes a farm-fresh selection of spiralized vegetables in the distinctive flavors of a fresh orange tarragon dressing.

Tips

If you do not have fresh oranges on hand, you can use 3 tbsp (45 mL) bottled orange juice in the dressing and omit the orange zest and slices.

This salad can be covered and refrigerated for up to 24 hours before serving.

▶ **Blender**

4	carrots, peeled and ends cut flat	4
3	broccoli stems, peeled	3
1	small head green cabbage, outer leaves removed and ends cut flat	1
2 tbsp	chopped fresh tarragon	30 mL
1 tbsp	¼-inch (0.5 cm) gingerroot pieces	15 mL
½ tsp	dry mustard	2 mL
1 tbsp	raw agave nectar	15 mL
	Grated zest and juice of 1 orange	
½ cup	cold-pressed extra virgin olive oil	125 mL
	Kosher salt	
	Freshly ground black pepper	
1	orange, peeled and sectioned	1

1. Using a spiralizer, cut carrots, broccoli and cabbage into thin strands. Transfer to a large bowl.

2. In blender, combine tarragon, ginger, mustard, agave nectar, orange zest and orange juice; pulse to combine. With the motor running, through the feed tube, gradually add oil, blending until combined. Season to taste with salt and pepper.

3. Drizzle dressing over carrot mixture and toss to combine. Top with orange slices. Let stand for 30 minutes before serving.

Carrot Pasta with Coconut Lime Dressing

This creamy citrus-and-coconut-imbued salad features sweet carrots and a whisper of licorice flavor from the fennel. Serve it as a satisfying main course with a light crispy green salad.

MAKES 4 TO 6 SERVINGS

Tips

When spiralizing, you always end up with a little bit of vegetable or fruit that is too small to spiralize. I use these pieces to taste-test my dressing before adding it to the salad.

Raw walnuts or hazelnuts are a nice substitution for the pistachios.

4	carrots, peeled and ends cut flat	4
2	turnips, peeled and ends cut flat	2
1	fennel bulb, peeled and ends cut flat	1
1 tbsp	grated gingerroot	15 mL
½ cup	coconut milk	125 mL
1 tbsp	tamari	15 mL
	Grated zest and juice of 1 lime	
	Kosher salt	
½ cup	chopped raw pistachios	125 mL
	Hot pepper flakes (optional)	

1. Using a spiralizer, cut carrots, turnips and fennel into thin strands. Transfer to a large bowl.

2. In a small bowl, whisk together ginger, coconut milk, tamari, lime zest and lime juice. Season to taste with salt.

3. Drizzle dressing over carrot mixture and toss to combine. Add pistachios and toss to combine. Sprinkle with hot pepper flakes (if using).

Tangled Carrot, Daikon and Sesame Salad

This lively, company-worthy salad has so much character, with its bold flavors and inviting vinaigrette! Top it with a protein or a cooked ingredient for guests who are not on a raw food diet.

MAKES 6 SERVINGS

Tips

Pea shoots can be found at Asian markets or local farmers' markets. They add the spring-fresh taste of baby peas to this dish. If you have trouble finding them, they can be omitted.

Apple ribbons quickly turn brown. If desired, you can spritz the ribbons lightly with lemon juice before adding them to the salad.

4	carrots, peeled and ends cut flat	4
4	broccoli stems, peeled and ends cut flat	4
1	daikon radish, peeled and ends cut flat	1
1	small head red cabbage, outer leaves removed and ends cut flat	1
5	green onions, thinly sliced diagonally	5
4 cups	baby pea shoots (see tip, at left)	1 L
1	clove garlic, minced	1
2 tsp	grated gingerroot	10 mL
¼ cup	cider vinegar	60 mL
1 tbsp	freshly squeezed lime juice	15 mL
2 tsp	raw liquid honey	10 mL
Dash	raw hot pepper sauce	Dash
⅔ cup	cold-pressed sesame oil	150 mL
1	crisp, tart apple (such as Braeburn or Granny Smith), cored and ends cut flat	1
	Chopped fresh cilantro (optional)	
	Hot pepper flakes (optional)	

1. Using a spiralizer, cut carrots, broccoli stems, radish and cabbage into thin strands.
2. In a large bowl, combine spiralized vegetables, green onions and pea shoots.
3. In a medium bowl, whisk together garlic, ginger, vinegar, lime juice, honey and hot pepper sauce. Gradually whisk in oil until combined.
4. Drizzle dressing over salad and toss to combine. Let stand for 5 minutes to blend the flavors, or cover and refrigerate for up to 3 hours.
5. Using a spiralizer, cut apple into wide ribbons. Arrange ribbons decoratively over salad. If desired, garnish with cilantro and hot pepper flakes.

Jicama and Watermelon Salad

You know it's summer when chin-dripping watermelons find their way to your table. For a light snack or side dish everyone will love, this combination of jicama and watermelon is a must-have for your next picnic.

Tip

Nigella seeds are a favorite in Middle Eastern and Indian cuisines. They add a subtle nutty onion flavor to dishes. They can be used as topping for many salads and vegetable dishes. Look for them in specialty markets or the Indian food section of well-stocked grocery stores. If you can't find them, chia seeds or raw shelled hemp seeds would make a good substitute.

1	jicama, peeled and ends cut flat	1
6 cups	cubed seedless watermelon (2-inch/5 cm cubes)	1.5 L
1 cup	torn fresh cilantro	250 mL
2 tsp	kosher salt	10 mL
1/2 cup	freshly squeezed lime juice	125 mL
2 tsp	nigella seeds (optional)	10 mL

1. Using a spiralizer, cut jicama into medium strands. Trim to varying lengths, as desired, and pat dry.

2. In a large bowl, combine jicama, watermelon, cilantro, salt and lime juice. Gently toss to coat. Sprinkle with nigella seeds (if using).

Parsnip Spaghetti with Pine Nut Basil Pesto

Delectably sweet parsnips make an inviting platform for creamy basil pesto.

Tips

If your spiralizer has a fine blade, you can cut the parsnips into fine strands for noodles that resemble angel-hair spaghetti.

Parsnips darken quickly once they are cut, so be sure to add the oil and lemon juice immediately.

▶ **Small food processor**

3	parsnips, peeled and ends cut flat	3
¼ cup	cold-pressed extra virgin olive oil, divided	60 mL
3 tbsp	freshly squeezed lemon juice, divided	45 mL
	Kosher salt	
1	clove garlic, minced	1
1 cup	packed fresh basil	250 mL
2 tbsp	raw pine nuts	30 mL
	Freshly ground black pepper	

1. Using a spiralizer, cut parsnips into thin strands.
2. In a large bowl, combine parsnips, 1 tbsp (15 mL) oil, 2 tbsp (30 mL) lemon juice and 1 tsp (5 mL) salt, tossing to coat. Set aside.
3. In food processor, combine garlic, basil, pine nuts and the remaining lemon juice; process until smooth. With the motor running, through the feed tube, gradually add the remaining oil, processing until combined.
4. Add pesto to parsnip mixture and toss to coat. Season to taste with salt and pepper.

Butternut Squash Noodles with Sun-Dried Tomatoes

Sun-dried tomatoes, fresh heirloom tomatoes and herbes de Provence coalesce into a creamy, scrumptious sauce that adds just the right touch to this favorite fall squash.

Tip

The bulbous end of the butternut squash contains seeds, so it does not spiralize well. Try roasting it instead, for a luscious side dish with any meal. Peel the squash, remove seeds and cut into 1½-inch (4 cm) cubes. Toss with melted butter, brown sugar, salt and pepper and roast in a 400°F (200°C) oven for 20 to 25 minutes.

▶ **Food processor**

1	butternut squash neck (at least 4 inches/10 cm long)	1
⅔ cup	cold-pressed avocado oil, divided	150 mL
1 tsp	salt, divided	5 mL
4	heirloom tomatoes, quartered	4
2	cloves garlic, minced	2
½ cup	drained oil-packed sun-dried tomatoes	125 mL
2 tsp	dried herbes de Provence	10 mL
¼ tsp	freshly ground black pepper	1 mL
1 tbsp	freshly squeezed lemon juice	15 mL

1. Peel squash neck and trim to 4 inches (10 cm) long, with flat ends. Using a spiralizer, cut squash into thin strands.

2. In a large bowl, combine squash, 2 tbsp (30 mL) oil and ½ tsp (2 mL) salt, tossing to coat. Let stand for 15 minutes or until softened to desired tenderness.

3. In food processor, combine quartered tomatoes, garlic, sun-dried tomatoes, herbes de Provence, pepper, the remaining salt and lemon juice; process for 30 seconds. With the motor running, through the feed tube, gradually add the remaining oil, processing for 1 minute or until creamy.

4. Drizzle dressing over squash and toss to combine.

Sweet Potato Noodle, Spinach and Walnut Salad

Sweet potato noodles take the forefront in this delicate spinach salad punctuated by a zesty mustard vinaigrette and crunchy walnuts.

MAKES 4 SERVINGS

Tip

Choose an olive oil that is cold-pressed. Many other olive-pressing methods can cause the olives to reach higher temperatures than desired in a raw food diet.

3	sweet potatoes, peeled and ends cut flat	3
1/3 cup	cold-pressed extra virgin olive oil, divided	75 mL
1/2 tsp	kosher salt	2 mL
1	clove garlic, minced	1
1 tsp	dry mustard	5 mL
2 tbsp	sherry vinegar	30 mL
4 cups	small spinach leaves	1 L
3	green onions, thinly sliced	3
1/2 cup	coarsely chopped raw walnuts	125 mL

1. Using a spiralizer, cut sweet potatoes into thin strands.

2. In a medium bowl, combine sweet potatoes, 3 tbsp (45 mL) oil and salt, tossing to coat. Let stand for 15 minutes or until softened to desired tenderness.

3. In a jar with a tight-fitting lid, combine garlic, mustard, the remaining oil and vinegar. Cover tightly and shake to combine.

4. In a large bowl, combine spinach and green onions. Drizzle with dressing and toss to combine. Top with sweet potatoes and walnuts.

Root Vegetable Salad with Orange Cumin Dressing

This invigorating salad combines sweet, tangy and crunchy root vegetables with a citrus dressing that has warm and nutty undertones. If you have never eaten raw turnips, get ready for a sweet, juicy and crisp treat.

MAKES 4 SERVINGS

Tips

Choose young carrots and turnips to get the ideal combination of flavors and textures. Older turnips can be chewy and will not have the perfect sweetness and tang of young turnips.

You can eat this salad immediately if you like, though the dressing will not have had time to work its magic of blending flavors and softening the vegetables. If you do eat it right away, you can skip the step of transferring the turnip ribbons to cold water.

> **Mortar and pestle**

3	carrots, peeled and ends cut flat	3
2	turnips, peeled and ends cut flat	2
	Cold water	
1	clove garlic, coarsely chopped	1
1	shallot, minced	1
½ tsp	kosher salt	2 mL
½ tsp	ground cumin	2 mL
¼ tsp	freshly ground black pepper	1 mL
⅓ cup	freshly squeezed orange juice	75 mL
3 tbsp	freshly squeezed lime juice	45 mL
1 tsp	raw agave nectar	5 mL
½ cup	cold-pressed extra virgin olive oil	125 mL
2 cups	packed arugula	500 mL
	Coarsely chopped fresh flat-leaf (Italian) parsley	

1. Using a spiralizer, cut carrots and 1⅔ turnips into thin strands. Cut the remaining turnip into wide ribbons. Transfer ribbons to a bowl of cold water to prevent discoloration.

2. Using a mortar and pestle, grind garlic, shallot, salt and cumin into a paste.

3. In a small bowl, whisk together garlic paste, pepper, orange juice, lime juice and agave nectar. Gradually whisk in oil until combined.

4. In a large bowl, combine arugula, carrots and thin turnip strands. Add dressing and toss to combine. Let stand for 30 minutes to blend the flavors and soften vegetables. Just before serving, drain turnip ribbons and arrange on top of the salad, then sprinkle with parsley.

Sprouted Quinoa with Twisted Carrots and Beets

This superpower salad boasts a bounty of palate-pleasing ingredients that are dressed to impress with a pistachio lime dressing.

MAKES 4 TO 6 SERVINGS

Tip

Choose carrots that are as straight as you can find to make it easier to cut them in your spiralizer. Thicker carrots work best, but choose those that are just large, not overgrown. Older, overgrown carrots take on a woody flavor.

▸ **Food processor**

3	yellow beets, with greens separated, ends cut flat	3
3	carrots, peeled and ends cut flat	3
1	sweet onion (such as Vidalia), peeled and ends cut flat	1
1 cup	sprouted quinoa (see box, page 203)	250 mL
3 tbsp	fresh parsley	45 mL
½ cup	cold-pressed extra virgin olive oil	125 mL
3 tbsp	freshly squeezed lime juice	45 mL
1 tbsp	raw agave nectar	15 mL
⅓ cup	raw pistachios	75 mL
	Water	
	Kosher salt	
	Freshly ground black pepper (optional)	

1. Using a spiralizer, cut beets and carrots into medium strands. Cut onion into thin strands. Trim all strands to desired length.

2. In a large bowl, combine spiralized vegetables and quinoa.

3. In food processor, combine parsley, oil, lime juice and agave nectar; process until smooth. Add pistachios and pulse until finely chopped but not smooth. If a thinner consistency is desired, add water, a little at a time, pulsing to combine. Season to taste with salt.

4. Drizzle dressing over quinoa mixture and toss to coat.

5. Trim stems from beet greens. Arrange leaves on individual serving plates and top with quinoa mixture. Sprinkle with pepper (if using).

Lettuce Wraps with Pineapple, Curly Jicama and Water Chestnuts

These hearty lettuce wraps are filled with a spicy walnut crumble, tomatoes, sweet and tangy fruits and fresh water chestnuts for a mouthwatering main course.

MAKES 6 SERVINGS

Tips

Chinese five-spice powder is readily available in grocery stores. It is a blend of ground cinnamon, cloves, fennel seeds, star anise and Szechuan peppercorns. You can make your own by grinding equal amounts of these ingredients (or adjusting the proportions to your taste).

Raw water chestnuts can be found in specialty food stores or Asian markets. They are well worth the effort, as they add a crunch and exotic sweetness to this dish. They must be peeled and washed thoroughly before use. If you can't find them, Jerusalem artichokes work as a substitute; use about 3 tbsp (45 mL) chopped.

▶ **Food processor**

1½ cups	chopped raw walnuts	375 mL
1 tbsp	Chinese five-spice powder	15 mL
1 tsp	tamari	5 mL
1½ tbsp	cold-pressed sesame oil	22 mL
Pinch	cayenne pepper	Pinch
Pinch	kosher salt	Pinch
1	jicama, peeled and ends cut flat	1
6	large lettuce leaves (such as romaine or iceberg)	6
4	raw water chestnuts, coarsely chopped	4
2	green onions, sliced diagonally	2
1	tomato, chopped	1
½ cup	chopped fresh pineapple	125 mL
½	avocado, mashed (optional)	½
	Raw hot pepper sauce (optional)	

1. Place walnuts in a medium bowl and cover with water. Let soak for 30 minutes or until fully softened. Drain and discard water. Rinse walnuts until water runs clear.

2. In food processor, combine walnuts, five-spice powder and tamari; process until mixture resembles ground meat. Through the feed tube, gradually add oil, pulsing to combine and to your desired texture. Season with cayenne and salt. Set aside.

3. Using a spiralizer, cut jicama into thin strands and pat dry.

4. Place a lettuce leaf on each of six serving plates. Top with walnut mixture, jicama, water chestnuts, green onions, tomato and pineapple. Roll lettuce around filling. If desired, serve with avocado and hot pepper sauce.

Spiralized Fruit Tarts

While I often think of tarts as a dessert item, I love to nibble on these little delights for breakfast or as an afternoon snack. Whenever you choose to enjoy them, you will want to make them again and again.

MAKES 6 SERVINGS

Tip

Apples start to discolor very quickly, so if you are not using the strands immediately, either spray them lightly with lemon juice or cover them with a mixture of 2 cups (500 mL) water and 1 tbsp (15 mL) lemon juice. Drain before use.

▸ **Food processor**
▸ **6-cup muffin pan, cups lined with plastic wrap**

6	pitted soft dates	6
2 cups	raw walnut halves or pieces	500 mL
¼ tsp	kosher salt, divided	1 mL
3 tbsp	raw agave nectar, divided	45 mL
4	crisp, tart apples (such as Cameo or Cortland), peeled, cored and ends cut flat	4
½ tsp	ground cinnamon	2 mL
Pinch	ground nutmeg	Pinch
2 tsp	freshly squeezed lemon juice	10 mL

1. In food processor, combine dates and walnuts; process until crumbly and sticky. Add a pinch of salt and 1 tbsp (15 mL) agave nectar; process until dough forms a ball.

2. Divide dough into six equal pieces and press one piece into the bottom and halfway up the sides of each prepared muffin cup to form a crust. Refrigerate.

3. Using a spiralizer, cut apples into thin strands.

4. In a medium bowl, combine apples, cinnamon, nutmeg, the remaining salt, the remaining agave nectar and lemon juice. Let stand for 30 minutes or until apples are softened to desired consistency.

5. Remove muffin pan from refrigerator. Remove tarts from pan and discard any liquid. Using tongs, divide apple strands among crusts, twisting them to fit.

Variations

Substitute firm pears (such as green or red Anjou) for the apples. Or use a combination of apples and pears. You will need 4 fruits total.

In place of the muffin pan, you can use four 3- by 1-inch (7.5 by 2.5 cm) mini tartlet pans. Divide the dough into four equal pieces and press one piece into the bottom and all the way up the sides of each tartlet pan.

Index

Library and Archives Canada Cataloguing in Publication

Haugen, Marilyn, author
      150 best spiralizer recipes / Marilyn Haugen & Jennifer Williams.

Includes index.
ISBN 978-0-7788-0522-9 (paperback)

1. Cooking (Vegetables). 2. Grinding machines. 3. Cookbooks.
I. Williams, Jennifer (Cookbook author), author
II. Title. III. Title: One hundred fifty best spiralizer recipes.

TX801.H39 2015   641.6'5   C2015-904297-6